Understanding Computers and Cognition

Understanding Computers and Cognition

A
New
Foundation
for Design

TERRY WINOGRAD
FERNANDO FLORES

Addison-Wesley Publishing Company, Inc.

Reading, Massachusetts   Menlo Park, California   New York
Don Mills, Ontario   Wokingham, England   Amsterdam   Bonn
Sydney   Singapore   Tokyo   Madrid   San Juan

ISBN: 0-201-11297-3

Originally published by Ablex Corporation, Norwood, NJ

Cover design by Copenhaver Cumpston

DEFGHIJ-HA-89

Fourth printing, January 1990

Contents

PART II – Computation, Thought, and Language

PART III – Design

For the people of Chile

Preface

This is a book about the design of computer technology. In it, we look closely at computers as they exist today and we set out new directions for future development. The discourse presented here, however, is not what one would expect to find in a book of science and engineering. It moves among topics and purposes that appear to be worlds apart: it is both theoretical and practical; it is concerned with computer technology and with the nature of human existence; with the philosophy of language and with office automation. But it is more than a study in contrasts. Our intention in bringing together these diverse elements is to generate understanding—to let the apparent chasms become spaces in which new possibilities are revealed.

All new technologies develop within the background of a tacit understanding of human nature and human work. The use of technology in turn leads to fundamental changes in what we do, and ultimately in what it is to be human. We encounter the deep questions of design when we recognize that in designing tools we are designing ways of being. By confronting these questions directly, we can develop a new background for understanding computer technology—one that can lead to important advances in the design and use of computer systems.

When we began the collaboration that led to this book, we had no idea where our discussions would lead. We had lived through very different experiences; we spoke different languages (both literally and metaphorically); and we had studied in disparate fields. Terry Winograd has been actively engaged for many years in computer science and artificial intelligence research at the Massachusetts Institute of Technology, Stanford University, and the Xerox Palo Alto Research Center. His work has consisted primarily of designing systems (both formal languages and computer programs) for the representation and analysis of language and knowledge. Fernando Flores has had experience with social and political organization at the highest level of government, in his posts as director of the state-owned corporations, Minister of Economics, and Minister of Finance in the government of Salvador Allende in Chile between 1970 and 1973. He was instrumental in a large-scale project to apply cybernetic theory to practical management problems (see Beer, *Platform for Change*, 1975) and is primarily interested in the understanding of social reality that we can gain through combining theory and practice. In spite of these differences, we had a sense that we shared much in our understanding of the world, and we entered into a dialog to explore this common ground. The dialog evolved into a paper, the paper in turn expanded and became a book, and the book evolved through a series of drafts whose focus shifted dramatically.

In our reading and discussions, we came to the realization that although our formal training was in the technical fields of mathematics and computer science, many of our guiding intuitions about language and thought were not compatible with the traditions in those disciplines. We found ourselves in much closer accord with writers who were far removed from the mathematico-logical paradigm, who identified their interests as *biology, hermeneutics*, and *phenomenology*. One of the initial attractions of this work was the understanding it provided of the larger human context in which the study of cognition has meaning. What surprised us was that the ideas were so relevant to the practical work in which we are engaged: the design of computer systems and the management of complex organizations. The philosophical ideas of thinkers such as Heidegger, Gadamer, Maturana, and Austin provided a framework to integrate what we had previously learned through our practical experience.

As we studied further, we began to formulate new theoretical foundations for the design of computer technologies. In working to clarify the nature and role of computers we were forced to reject many assumptions that we had long accepted implicitly and that go unquestioned in most discussions of computing. We had to address new questions, and these in turn led to looking more carefully at what people actually *do* with computers, and what might be done better.

Readers with a background in science and technology may find it implausible that philosophical considerations have practical relevance for their work. Philosophy may be an amusing diversion, but it seems that the theories relevant to technological development are those of the hard sciences and engineering. We have found quite the opposite. Theories about the nature of biological existence, about language, and about the nature of human action have a profound influence on the shape of what we build and how we use it. We have accordingly devoted a considerable amount of space, especially in the first part of the book, to discussing matters that appear unrelated to computers but that are nonetheless indispensable in the process of opening up for the reader new possibilities and new directions for what we can do with them.

In the course of developing a new understanding we came across questions that have long been the subject of debate, such as "Can computers think?", "Can computers understand language?", and "What is rational decision-making?" We address these questions not so much to solve them as to *dissolve* them. They arise in a background of understanding about human thought and language, a background that itself needs to be re-examined and revised. In the end, we are not concerned with providing new answers to questions about technology as they have traditionally been posed. We look towards new questions that can lead to the design and use of machines that are suited to human purposes.

Our book is intended for a wide audience—not just those who are professionally involved in computer research, design, and production, or scholars working in related fields such as cognitive psychology, linguistics, and management science. We address everyone (expert and layperson alike) who has a serious interest in understanding what computers are and how they fit into our lives.

Although we devote a good deal of attention to philosophical background, we have not attempted to make this a scholarly book. Our intention is to lead the reader through some of the intellectual pathways that shaped our own understanding, and this process is by necessity selective. We do not attempt to trace historical antecedents, to assign proper credit for originality, or to point out the many other thinkers who have dealt with the same topics in related ways. In fact, much of what we cite is from books intended to provide popularized accounts and from articles appearing in the popular press. The concern about what computers can do is not an abstract conundrum to be puzzled over for intellectual amusement, but a practical question at the center of a significant discourse in society as a whole. The answer as understood by the public (including those who make political and business decisions) is ultimately more significant than the twists and turns of academic debate. By dealing with the understanding that appears in the public discourse about computing, we can better achieve what we have set out to do—to reveal the pre-understanding we and others bring to computer technology and by doing so to open a new clearing in which to glimpse future paths for design.

Acknowledgments

In developing this book over a number of years, we have benefited from discussions with many people, including Jean Bamberger, Chauncey Bell, Daniel Bobrow, Aaron Cicourel, Werner Erhard, Michael Graves, Heinz von Foerster, Anatol Holt, Rob Kling, George Lakoff, Juan Ludlow, Donald Norman, Donald Schon, John Searle, Francisco Varela, and students in a series of seminars at Stanford University. We are especially grateful to Ralph Cherubini, Hubert Dreyfus, Anne Gardner, Elihu Gerson,

Humberto Maturana, Brian Smith, Peter Stokoe, and Paul Trachtman for extended and insightful commentaries on earlier drafts. Our dialogs with them have been the source of much of our understanding, and we appreciate their efforts and concern. Richard Ogle's probing discussion and editorial assistance were vital to the completion of the manuscript.

This work was made possible by support to Terry Winograd from the System Development Foundation and from Stanford University's Center for the Study of Language and Information. We owe profound gratitude to those people at Stanford and in Amnesty International whose efforts made freedom possible for Fernando Flores. These include George Dantzig, Richard Fagen, Robert Floyd, and Charles Meyer.

Finally, we want to acknowledge the people of Chile for their courage to open new conversations for possibility and for their strength in times of trial. From them we have learned much about language, about meaning, and about living.

Terry Winograd
Fernando Flores

Palo Alto, California
July, 1985

PART I

Theoretical Background

Chapter 1

Introduction

Computers are everywhere. The versatile silicon chip has found a place in our homes, our schools, our work, and our leisure. We must cope with a flood of new devices, bringing with them both benefits and dangers. Popular books and magazines proclaim that we are witnessing a 'computer revolution,' entering a 'micro-millennium' in which computers will completely transform our lives.

We search for images that can help us anticipate computer impacts and direct further development. Are computers merely giant adding machines or are they electronic brains? Can they only do 'programmed' rote tasks or can we expect them to learn and create? The popular discourse about these questions draws heavily on the analogy between computation and human thought:

> While many areas of human endeavor have currently seemed to flounder—such as understanding and dealing with economic systems or correcting social injustices—research and technical developments in the scientific field of artificial intelligence have exploded.... As a result, artificial-intelligence researchers are developing computers that can listen to spoken sentences and grasp their meaning; that can read news stories and write succinct, accurate, grammatical summaries; that employ robots, who never get bored, to work on assembly lines; that assemble data about a sick person—and suggest a diagnosis.— Stockton, "Creating computers to think like humans" (1980), p. 41.

> In five or six years—by 1988 or thereabouts—portable, quasi-human brains, made of silicon or gallium arsenide, will be commonplace. They will be an intelligent electronic race, working

3

as partners with the human race. We will carry these small creatures around with us everywhere. Just pick them up, tuck them under your arm, and go off to attend to your business. They will be Artoo-Deetoos without wheels: brilliant, but nice personalities, never sarcastic, always giving you a straight answer—little electronic friends that can solve all your problems. — Jastrow, "The thinking computer" (1982), p. 107.

We are about to embark on a massive programme to develop highly intelligent machines, a process by which we will lead computers by the hand until they reach our own intellectual level, after which they will proceed to surpass us.... But what will we do with the Ultra-Intelligent Machines when they arrive? Clearly, the first thing would be to put them to work on some of the numerous problems facing society. These could be economic, medical or educational matters, and also, perhaps, strategic modelling to forecast trends and produce early warnings of difficulties or crises.... It is unlikely that there will be any serious objections to this apart from those of an emotional or doctrinaire nature. — Evans, *The Micro Millennium* (1979), pp. 195-196, 229.

But focussing on the image of 'computer as brain' can lead us away from the important questions. The concern with giving computers human-like (or god-like) intelligence rests on a more fundamental discourse about the nature of technology and of human thinking, language, and being. This discourse has unfolded within a tradition—a way of understanding—that is deeply rooted in modern technological society.

In examining this tradition, we came to realize that although it provides a fertile background for developing new technology, it does not support an adequate understanding of what computer devices *do* in a context of human practice. We were led to a broad critique of what has been said about computers, and what has been done in disciplines such as linguistics, psychology, and management science. We developed a new orientation that provides an alternative basis for understanding computer technology.

1.1   The question of design

In order to understand the phenomena surrounding a new technology, we must open the question of *design*—the interaction between understanding and creation. In speaking here of design, we are not restricting our concern to the methodology of conscious design. We address the broader question of how a society engenders inventions whose existence in turn alters that society. We need to establish a theoretical basis for looking at what the devices do, not just how they operate.

In order to develop such a theoretical basis we must step back and examine the implicit understanding of design that guides technological development within our existing tradition of thought. Only by unconcealing that tradition and making explicit its assumptions can we open ourselves to alternatives and to the new design possibilities that flow from them. The remainder of this introduction provides a guide to how we have undertaken that task in this book.

We can illustrate the kind of questioning we have in mind by seriously asking "What is a word processor?" The first thing to recognize is that different answers grow from the concerns of different individuals. For the manager of a factory that builds word processors, they are assemblies of electronic and mechanical devices, to be constructed, tested, and shipped. For the person who programs the word processor, it is a particular collection of software, dealing with the input, storage, and output of bytes of information. It operates through some kind of interface to a user who generates and modifies that information.

These are both perfectly valid answers, arising in particular domains to which the theories of computation and electronics are relevant. If we want to understand a breakdown of the hardware or software, we operate in their terms and turn to them for predictions. But these answers do not deal with what a word processor *does*—with the fact that it is a medium for the creation and modification of linguistic structures that play a role in human communication. For the purchaser of a word processor, this is the relevant domain. The word processor exists as a collection of hardware or programs only when it breaks down.[1] In its use, one is concerned with the actions of creating and modifying documents and producing physical presentations of them on a screen or printed page. The relevant domain is not a computational one, but one that emerged long ago with the first writing instruments. It brings with it concerns of visual presentation—issues of layout, type fonts, and integration of text with illustrations. Many current computer products are designed with a primary concern for this domain. They deal at length with formats and typography, focussing on the document as the thing being produced.

But still with this, we have not reached a full understanding of the word processor. We cannot take the activity of writing as an independent phenomenon. Writing is an instrument—a tool we use in our interactions with other people. The computer, like any other medium, must be understood in the context of communication and the larger network of equipment and

---

[1] As we will see in later chapters, this includes the initial breakdown implicit in the condition of *unreadiness* that calls for buying and assembling a new system.

practices in which it is situated. A person who sits down at a word processor is not just creating a document, but is writing a letter or a memo or a book. There is a complex social network in which these activities make sense. It includes institutions (such as post offices and publishing companies), equipment (including word processors and computer networks, but also all of the older technologies with which they coexist), practices (such as buying books and reading the daily mail), and conventions (such as the legal status of written documents).

The significance of a new invention lies in how it fits into and changes this network. Many innovations are minor—they simply improve some aspect of the network without altering its structure. The automatic transmission made automobiles easier to use, but did not change their role. Other inventions, such as the computer, are radical innovations that cannot be understood in terms of the previously existing network. The printing press, the automobile, and television are all examples of radical innovations that opened up whole new domains of possibilities for the network of human interactions. Just as the automobile had impacts on our society far beyond speeding up what had been done with horses, the use of computers will lead to changes far beyond those of a fancy typewriter. The nature of publishing, the structure of communication within organizations, and the social organization of knowledge will all be altered, as they were with the emergence of other technologies for language, such as the printing press.

One might think that the questioning can stop at this point. It is clear (and has been widely recognized) that one cannot understand a technology without having a *functional* understanding of how it is used. Furthermore, that understanding must incorporate a *holistic* view of the network of technologies and activities into which it fits, rather than treating the technological devices in isolation. But this is still not enough. We can say that the word processor must be understood by virtue of the role it plays in communication, the distribution of information, and the accumulation of knowledge. But in doing so we take for granted the use of words like 'communication,' 'information,' and 'knowledge,' which themselves require closer examination. In this examination, we find ourselves being drawn into inquiries about basic human phenomena that have been called things like 'intelligence,' 'language,' and 'rationality.'

As the use of a new technology changes human practices, our ways of speaking about that technology change our language and our understanding. This new way of speaking in turn creates changes in the world we construct. As an example of how new language creates new possibilities for action, consider Freud's introduction of terms such as 'ego,' 'subconscious,' and 'repression.' At one level we might say that he recognized and labelled phenomena that had always existed. But the innovation in his language had a major impact on human society, in everything from the way we treat deviants (such as prisoners and the mentally ill) to the way we teach our children.

Looking at computers we find the same process at work. The development of the technology has led to new uses of terms such as 'information,' 'input,' 'output,' 'language,' and 'communication,' while work in areas such as artificial intelligence is bringing new meanings to words like 'intelligence,' 'decision,' and 'knowledge.' The technical jargon gives shape to our commonsense understanding in a way that changes our lives.

In order to become aware of the effects that computers have on society we must reveal the implicit understanding of human language, thought, and work that serves as a background for developments in computer technology. In this endeavor we are doubly concerned with language. First, we are studying a technology that operates in a domain of language. The computer is a device for creating, manipulating, and transmitting symbolic (hence linguistic) objects. Second, in looking at the impact of the computer, we find ourselves thrown back into questions of language—how practice shapes our language and language in turn generates the space of possibilities for action.

This book, then, is permeated by a concern for language. Much of our theory is a theory of language, and our understanding of the computer centers on the role it will play in mediating and facilitating linguistic action as the essential human activity. In asking what computers can do, we are drawn into asking what people do with them, and in the end into addressing the fundamental question of what it means to be human.

1.2 The role of tradition

One cannot approach questions like those raised in the previous section from a neutral or objective standpoint. Every questioning grows out of a *tradition*—a pre-understanding that opens the space of possible answers. We use the word 'tradition' here in a broad sense, without the connotation that it belongs to a cohesive social or cultural group, or that it consists of particular customs or practices. It is a more pervasive, fundamental phenomenon that might be called a 'way of being.' In trying to understand a tradition, the first thing we must become aware of is how it is concealed by its obviousness. It is not a set of rules or sayings, or something we will find catalogued in an encyclopedia. It is a way of understanding, a background, within which we interpret and act. We use the word 'tradition' because it emphasizes the historicity of our ways of thinking—the fact that we always exist within a pre-understanding determined by the history of our interactions with others who share the tradition.

When we encounter people who live in a substantially different tradition, we are struck by the impression that they have a strange and apparently arbitrary 'world view.' It takes a careful self-awareness to turn the same gaze on our own lives and 'unconceal' our own tradition—to bring into conscious observation that which invisibly gives shape to our thought.

In examining how people have thought about and talked about computers, we become aware of the pervasive effect of a powerful tradition that emphasizes 'information,' 'representation,' and 'decision making.' This tradition has been the basis for a great deal of technological progress and it has also led to many of the problems created by the use of computers. Even in discussions of what computers can and cannot do, the questions that are posed reflect a particular blindness about the nature of human thought and language—a blindness that can lead to a broad misunderstanding of the role that will be played by computers.

We have labelled this tradition the 'rationalistic tradition' because of its emphasis on particular styles of consciously rationalized thought and action. In calling it 'rationalistic' we are not equating it with 'rational.' We are not interested in a defense of irrationality or a mystic appeal to nonrational intuition. The rationalistic tradition is distinguished by its narrow focus on certain aspects of rationality, which (as we will show throughout the book) often leads to attitudes and activities that are not rational when viewed in a broader perspective. Our commitment is to developing a new ground for rationality—one that is as rigorous as the rationalistic tradition in its aspirations but that does not share the presuppositions behind it.

The task we have undertaken in this book is to challenge the rationalistic tradition, introducing an alternative orientation that can lead to asking new questions. In developing this new orientation, we were led to a critique of the current mythology of artificial intelligence and its related cognitive theories, drawing conclusions that contradict the naive optimism apparent in the quotations at the beginning of the chapter. Our ultimate goal, however, is not a debunking but a redirection. The alternative we pose is not a position in a debate about whether or not computers will be intelligent, but an attempt to create a new understanding of how to design computer tools suited to human use and human purposes.

1.3 Our path

Our intention is to provide an opportunity for the reader to develop a new orientation. No book can embody the result of such a process, but through entering a dialog with the reader we can help make it possible. We have attempted to do this in three steps. First we present some previous work that challenges the theoretical assumptions of the rationalistic tradition, calling into question much of what is normally taken for granted in our tradition. Next we carefully examine, from the orientation developed in the first part, the phenomena that have emerged in the practice of computer technology. Finally, we suggest some alternative directions for the design of computer-based tools.

Part I of the book (Chapters 1-6) describes the rationalistic tradition and presents three distinct bodies of work, each of which stands in contrast to that tradition and each of which has deeply influenced our own understanding. We do not attempt to provide a philosophical exposition and critique in which arguments for and against each position are enumerated and weighed. We find it more fruitful to present the central points, listening for their relevance to our own concerns. Our discourse is theoretical in that it deals with fundamental questions, but it is not directed towards postulating formal theories that can be systematically used to make predictions. As will become clear, one of the most prominent illusions of the rationalistic tradition is the belief that knowledge consists of explicit theories of that sort.

Chapter 2 describes the rationalistic tradition in some detail, showing how it serves as a basis for our culture's commonsense understanding of language, thought, and rationality. Our goal is to reveal biases and assumptions that are concealed by their embodiment in the background of our language.

Chapter 3 deals with a tradition that includes *hermeneutics* (the study of interpretation) and *phenomenology* (the philosophical examination of the foundations of experience and action). This tradition has emerged from humanistic studies, and is concerned with the relation of the individual to the context—especially the social context—in which he or she lives. It emphasizes those areas of human experience where individual interpretation and intuitive understanding (as opposed to logical deduction and conscious reflection) play a central role. Its exponents challenge the belief that a formal analytical understanding of these phenomena is possible at all.

We concentrate on the work of Hans-Georg Gadamer and Martin Heidegger. Many other philosophers have explored related ideas, including phenomenologists such as Husserl, Ricoeur, and Merleau-Ponty, existentialists such as Sartre, pragmatists such as Mead and Dewey, current political philosophers such as Habermas and Apel, and even some with a more analytic background, such as Wittgenstein. We have selected Heidegger and Gadamer, partly because of the role their writings played in our own learning, and partly because of their intrinsic importance within the tradition they represent. Heidegger stands out as the modern philosopher who has done the most thorough, penetrating, and radical analysis of everyday experience. His ideas lie at the root of much of what other philosophers have said, and at the root of our own orientation. Gadamer has been most articulate in applying this orientation to the problem of language, a problem that we see as central. Since it was not our intention to produce a work of philosophical scholarship, we do not attempt to draw connections between the discourse developed by these two philosophers and the many others that preceded and followed them. Our aim is to bring out the relevant distinctions in the clearest possible way, by focussing on their central insights.

Chapter 4 presents the work of Humberto R. Maturana, a Chilean neurobiologist most widely known for his work on the neurophysiology of vision. His background is that of a biologist, not a philosopher, and he deals first and foremost with the nature of biological organisms as *mechanistic structure-determined systems.* His work was critical in the development of our understanding of cognition and of our perspective on the rationalistic tradition.

Writers like Heidegger challenge the dominant view of mind, declaring that cognition is not based on the systematic manipulation of representations. This perspective has been the basis for several critiques of artificial intelligence[2] that initially have a kind of mystical feel to those within the scientific community. In questioning the common understanding of the relationship among perception, representation, and thought, these accounts seem at first sight to deny the physical basis of human action. Maturana provides two useful insights that let us escape from this limited pre-understanding: the role of the observer in creating *phenomenal domains;* and the concept of *structural coupling,* which allows us to understand behavior that is mechanically generated but not programmed. As a biologist, Maturana sets out a conceptual framework in which phenomena of interpretation arise as a necessary consequence of the structure of biological beings. At the same time, he compels us to acquire a new understanding of the way we talk about physical nature and to apply this understanding to ourselves.

As we pointed out earlier, questions concerning cognition are intertwined with questions about the nature of language. Chapter 5 begins by showing how the insights of hermeneutics are relevant to the issues that have traditionally been addressed by linguists and analytic philosophers of language. It emphasizes the role of the listener in the active generation of meaning, showing how the idealization of 'literal meaning' breaks down in looking at ordinary language. We then introduce speech act theory, as developed by Austin and Searle and later adapted by social philosophers such as Habermas. Although this work grew out of the analytic school of philosophy, its view of language as speech acts challenges the rationalistic

---

[2]For example, see Dreyfus, *What Computers Can't Do* (1979) and Haugeland, "The nature and plausibility of cognitivism" (1978).

tradition by suggesting that language, and therefore thought, is ultimately based on social interaction. Speech act theory is a starting point for an understanding of language as an act of social creation. In the last part of the chapter we present our own synthesis of speech act theory and the hermeneutic understanding of language developed in Chapter 3. This synthesis is central to our interpretation of computer technology in the second part of the book. It leads us to the conclusion that we create our world through language, an observation that has important consequences for design.

Chapter 6, which acts as a transition to the remainder of the book, draws out and summarizes some common points from the preceding three chapters. The rejection of cognition as the manipulation of knowledge of an objective world, the primacy of action and its central role in language, and the impossibility of completely articulating background assumptions all play a major role in the critique of current computer technology presented in Part II and in the new design orientation elaborated in Part III.

Part II (Chapters 7-10) addresses concrete questions about what computers do. Our goal is to understand and reinterpret what is currently being done and to anticipate future developments.

Chapter 7 describes what people do when they program computers. It focusses on the relationship between the intentions of programmers and the behavior of devices that run the programs they create. Programming is a process of creating symbolic representations that are to be interpreted at some level within a hierarchy of constructs of varying degrees of abstractness. The interactions between levels of representation can be complex, since each is implemented in terms of the lower ones. This description lays the groundwork for the discussion of computer intelligence in the following chapters.

Chapter 8 examines the computational techniques that have been proposed as a basis for artificial intelligence. Drawing on the ideas outlined in Part I, we argue—contrary to widespread current belief—that one cannot construct machines that either exhibit or successfully model intelligent behavior. We begin by asking why mind-like properties are attributed to computers but not to other types of machines that can equally be said to provide or process information. We continue with a more thorough exposition of work in artificial intelligence and an analysis of its limitations. Many of the difficulties with current research derive from a fundamental orientation that equates intelligence with rationalistic problem solving based on heuristic procedures.

Chapter 9 takes up the theme of the preceding chapter within the context of computer programs that process natural language. We look at why the many programs developed during the 1970s do not approach the human ability to interpret meaning. In spite of a wide variety of ingenious techniques for making analysis and recognition more flexible, the scope of comprehension remains severely limited. There may be practical applications for computer processing of natural-language-like formalisms and for limited processing of natural language, but computers will remain incapable of using language in the way human beings do, both in interpretation and in the generation of commitment that is central to language.

Chapter 10 takes a critical look at some major current research directions in areas such as knowledge engineering, expert systems, and the so-called 'fifth generation' computers. It describes the overall shift from the general goal of creating programs that can understand language and thought to that of designing software for specialized task domains, and evaluates the projections being made for the coming years.

Part III (Chapters 11 and 12) presents an alternative orientation to design, based on the theoretical background we have developed. The relevant questions are not those comparing computers to people, but those opening up a potential for computers that play a meaningful role in human life and work. Once we move away from the blindness generated by the old questions, we can take a broader perspective on what computers *can* do.

Chapter 11 addresses the task of designing computer tools for use in organizational contexts. We focus on the activity of people called 'managers,' but the same concerns arise in all situations involving social interaction and collaborative effort. Drawing on Heidegger's discussion of 'thrownness' and 'breakdown,' we conclude that models of rationalistic problem solving do not reflect how actions are really determined, and that programs based on such models are unlikely to prove successful. Nevertheless, there is a role for computer technology in support of managers and as aids in coping with the complex conversational structures generated within an organization. Much of the work that managers do is concerned with initiating, monitoring, and above all coordinating the networks of speech acts that constitute social action.

Chapter 12 returns to the fundamental questions of design and looks at possibilities for computer technology opened up by the understanding developed in the preceding chapters. After briefly reviewing the relevant theoretical ideas outlined earlier, we examine some of the phenomena to which design must address itself, illustrating our approach with a concrete example. We also consider design in relation to *systematic domains* of human activity, where the objects of concern are formal structures and the rules for manipulating them. The challenge posed here for design is not simply to create tools that accurately reflect existing domains, but to provide for the creation of new domains. Design serves simultaneously to bring forth and to transform the objects, relations, and regularities of the world of our concerns.

In one sense, then, this is a book about computers. But it reaches beyond the specific issues of what computers can do. Our larger goal is to clarify the background of understanding in which the discourse about computers and technology takes place, and to grasp its broader implications. Ultimately we are seeking a better understanding of what it means to be human. In this quest, progress is not made by finding the 'right answers,' but by asking meaningful questions—ones that evoke an openness to new ways of being. We invite the readers to create with us an openness that can alter our collective vision of how computer technology will develop in the coming decades.

Chapter 2

The rationalistic tradition

Current thinking about computers and their impact on society has been shaped by a rationalistic tradition that needs to be re-examined and challenged as a source of understanding. As a first step we will characterize the tradition of rationalism and logical empiricism that can be traced back at least to Plato. This tradition has been the mainspring of Western science and technology, and has demonstrated its effectiveness most clearly in the 'hard sciences'—those that explain the operation of deterministic mechanisms whose principles can be captured in formal systems. The tradition finds its highest expression in mathematics and logic, and has greatly influenced the development of linguistics and cognitive psychology.

We will make no attempt to provide a full historical account of this tradition, or to situate it on some kind of intellectual map. Instead, we have chosen to concentrate on understanding its effects on current discourse and practice, especially in relation to the development and impact of computers. The purpose of this chapter is to outline its major points and illustrate their embodiment in current theories of language, mind, and action.

2.1 The rationalistic orientation

We can begin to reveal the rationalistic tradition by considering the question "What do you do when faced with some problem whose solution you care about?" The rationalistic orientation can be depicted in a series of steps:

1. Characterize the situation in terms of identifiable objects with well-defined properties.

2. Find general rules that apply to situations in terms of those objects and properties.

3. Apply the rules logically to the situation of concern, drawing conclusions about what should be done.

There are obvious questions about how we set situations into correspondence with systematic 'representations' of objects and properties, and with how we can come to know general rules. In much of the rationalistic tradition, however, these are deferred in favor of emphasizing the formulation of systematic rules that can be used to draw logical conclusions. Much of Western philosophy—from classical rhetoric to modern symbolic logic—can be seen as a drive to come up with more systematic and precise formulations of just what constitutes valid reasoning.

Questions of correspondence and knowledge still exercise philosophers, but in the everyday discourse about thinking and reasoning they are taken as unproblematic. In fact when they are raised, the discussion is often characterized as being too philosophical. Even within philosophy, there are schools (such as analytic philosophy) in which the problems raised by the first two items are pushed aside, not because they are uninteresting, but because they are too difficult and open-ended. By concentrating on formalisms and logical rules, the philosopher can develop clear technical results whose validity can be judged in terms of internal coherence and consistency.

There is a close correlation between the rationalistic tradition and the approach of organized science. In a broad sense, we can view any organized form of inquiry as a science, but in ordinary usage more is implied. There must be some degree of adherence to the scientific method. This method consists of a series of basic steps (that can be repeated in successive refinements of the science):

> [The scientific method] can be described as involving the following operations: (a) observation of a phenomenon that, henceforth, is taken as a problem to be explained; (b) proposition of an explanatory hypothesis in the form of a deterministic system that can generate a phenomenon isomorphic with the one observed; (c) proposition of a computed state or process in the system specified by the hypothesis as a predicted phenomenon to be observed; and (d) observation of the predicted phenomenon.— Maturana, "Biology of language: The epistemology of reality" (1978), p. 28.

The scientist first notes some regularity in the phenomena of interest—some recurring pattern of observations. He or she proposes a conceptual or concrete system that can be set into correspondence with the observations and that can be manipulated to make predictions about other potential observations. Conditions are created in which these observations can be expected and the results used to modify the theory. Scientific research consists of setting up situations in which observable activity will be determined in a clear way by a small number of variables that can be systematically manipulated. This simplicity is necessary if the modelling system is to make predictions that can be checked.

The rationalistic orientation not only underlies both pure and applied science but is also regarded, perhaps because of the prestige and success that modern science enjoys, as the very paradigm of what it means to think and be intelligent. In studies of thought, emphasis is placed on the form of the rules and on the nature of the processes by which they are logically applied. Areas of mathematics, such as symbolic logic and automata theory, are taken as the basis for formalizing what goes on when a person perceives, thinks, and acts. For someone trained in science and technology it may seem self-evident that this is the right (or even the only) approach to serious thinking. Indeed, this is why many workers in artificial intelligence find critiques like that of Dreyfus (*What Computers Can't Do*, 1979) obviously wrong, since they challenge this deep-seated pre-understanding. In defense, they argue that the only conceivable alternative is some kind of mysticism, religion, or fuzzy thinking that is a throwback to earlier stages of civilization.

It is scarcely surprising, then, that the rationalistic orientation pervades not only artificial intelligence and the rest of computer science, but also much of linguistics, management theory, and cognitive science—three areas with which artificial intelligence has been closely associated. In the next three sections we will examine each of these areas in turn, seeing how rationalistic styles of discourse and thinking have determined the questions that have been asked and the theories, methodologies, and assumptions that have been adopted.

First, however, a caveat is in order. In presenting these elements as part of an overall rationalistic tradition, we are aware that they are not uniformly accepted in carefully reasoned work of analytic philosophers.[1] However it would be a mistake to therefore not take this tradition seriously. It pervades the work of those same philosophers and of researchers in

---

[1] In some ways, the rationalistic tradition might better be termed the 'analytic tradition.' We have adopted a more neutral label in order to avoid the impression that we are engaged in a philosophical debate in which philosophers labelled 'analytic' take the other side. We also are not concerned here with the debate between 'rationalists' and 'empiricists.' The rationalistic tradition spans work in both of these lines.

computer science and psychology as well. In moments of careful reflection they acknowledge the importance of phenomena that are not subject to the rationalistic style of analysis, but in their day-to-day work they proceed as though everything were. In generating theories and in building programs, they operate in a style that is fully consistent with the naive tradition and avoid areas in which it breaks down. In the end, we are really concerned not with the philosophical arguments, but with a broader phenomenon— the role of a tradition in giving orientation to people who do not consider themselves philosophers, but whose ways of thinking nevertheless embody a philosophical orientation.

2.2 Language, truth, and the world

Much of our book is an attempt to show the non-obviousness of the rationalistic orientation and to reveal the blindness that it generates. In pursuing this, we found ourselves deeply concerned with the question of language. The rationalistic tradition regards language as a system of symbols that are composed into patterns that stand for things in the world. Sentences can represent the world truly or falsely, coherently or incoherently, but their ultimate grounding is in their *correspondence* with the states of affairs they represent. This concept of correspondence can be summarized as:

1. Sentences say things about the world, and can be either true or false.

2. What a sentence says about the world is a function of the words it contains and the structures into which these are combined.

3. The content words of a sentence (such as its nouns, verbs, and adjectives) can be taken as denoting (in the world) objects, properties, relationships, or sets of these.

Of course most people will not be able to formulate these assumptions directly. For example, they may not be aware of the distinction between 'content words' (like "dog" and "disappear") and 'function words' (like "of" and "the"). But they would find none of these statements surprising or unintuitive.

The relation of these assumptions to more formal studies of semantics is more complex. During this century a large body of work has been produced that systematically examines meaning from a formal analytical perspective.[2] Its goal is to explain the regularities in the correspondence

---

[2] Analysis of this style was developed by such prominent philosophers and logicians as Frege (1949), Russell (1920), and Tarski (1944). More recent work is presented in

between what we say and what we mean. There are two levels at which to define the problem. First, there is the problem of 'semantic correspondence.' Just what is the relationship between a sentence (or a word) and the objects, properties, and relations we observe in the world? Few philosophers adhere to the naive view that one can assume the presence of an objective reality in which objects and their properties are 'simply there.' They recognize deep *ontological* problems in deciding just what constitutes a distinct object or in what sense a relation or event 'exists.' Some limited aspects (such as the reference of proper names) have been studied within the philosophy of language, but it is typically assumed that no formal answers can be given to the general problem of semantic correspondence.

The second, more tractable level at which to study meaning is to take for granted that *some* kind of correspondence exists, without making a commitment to its ontological grounding. Having done this, one can look at the *relations* among the meanings of different words, phrases, and sentences, without having to answer the difficult question of just what those meanings are.[3]

There are many different styles in which this study can be carried out. The approach called 'structural semantics' or 'linguistic semantics'[4] deals only with the linguistic objects (words, phrases, and sentences) themselves. The fact that "Sincerity admires John" is anomalous or that "male parent" and "father" are synonymous can be encompassed within a theory relating words (and posited features of words) to their occurrences in certain kinds of phrases and sentences. Within such a theory there need be no reference either to the act of uttering the words or to the states of affairs they describe.

This approach is limited, however, because of its dependence on specific words and structures as the basis for stating general rules. Most theories of semantics make use of a formalized language in which deeper regularities can be expressed. It is assumed that each sentence in a natural language (such as English) can be set into correspondence with one or more possible interpretations in a formal language (such as the first-order predicate calculus) for which the rules of reasoning are well defined. The study of meaning then includes both the translation of sentences into the corresponding formal structures and the logical rules associated with these structures. Thus the sentences "Every dog has a tail," "All dogs

---

several collections, such as Linsky (1952), Davidson and Harman (1972), Hintikka, Moravcsik, and Suppes (1973), and some of the papers in Keenan (1975).

[3] For a critique of recent attempts to extend this methodology, see Winograd, "Moving the semantic fulcrum" (1985).

[4] In this category, we include work such as that of Leech (1969), Lyons (1963), Katz and Fodor (1964), and Jackendoff (1976).

have tails," and "A dog has a tail" are all translated into the same form, while "I walked to the bank" will have two possible translations (corresponding to the two meanings of "bank"), as will "Visiting relatives can be boring" (corresponding to different interpretations of who is doing the visiting).

Most current work in this direction adopts some form of 'truth theoretic' characterization of meaning. We can summarize its underlying assumptions as follows:

1. There is a system of rules (which may include 'pragmatic' and contextual considerations) by which sentences of a natural language can be translated into formulas of a formal language, such that the essence of their meaning is preserved.

2. There is another system of rules by which the meanings of formulas in this formal language are determined in a systematic way by the meanings of their parts and the structures by which those parts are combined.

3. There are systematic rules of logic that account for the interrelation of the truth conditions for different formulas.

4. The fundamental kind of sentence is the indicative, which can be taken as stating that a certain proposition is true. Its meaning can be characterized in terms of the conditions in the world under which it would be true.

In addition to these assumptions, there is a general understanding that in order for the compositional rules to be of interest, the meanings of the items being composed should be fixed *without reference to the context in which they appear.* If the meaning of each item could vary arbitrarily with each use, the rules for composing meanings would be vacuous. There would be no systematic notion of a meaning of the item which applied to all of its uses. Of course, this context-independence cannot be taken as an absolute; there are obvious recognized exceptions.[5] But the central theory of meaning (semantics) deals with words and sentences in terms of their *literal meaning,* which is treated as not context-dependent. We will discuss the consequences of this assumption in Chapter 5.

The correspondence theory of language is one cornerstone on which other aspects of the rationalistic tradition rest. Rationalistic theories of

---

[5] These include indexical pronouns ("I," "you"), place and time adverbs ("here," "now"), and the use of tenses (as in "He will go."). It is also clearly understood that there are dependencies on the linguistic context (as with the anaphoric pronouns "he," "she," "it") and that there are metaphorical and poetic uses of language which depend on complex personal contexts.

mind all adopt some form of a 'representation hypothesis,' in which it is assumed that thought is the manipulation of representation structures in the mind. Although these representations are not specifically linguistic (that is, not the sentences of an ordinary human language), they are treated as sentences in an 'internal language,' whose connection to the world of the thinker follows the principles outlined above.

2.3   Decision making and problem solving

Another modern embodiment of the rationalistic tradition is in the discipline of management science, a field concerned with mathematical analyses of decision making and with behavioral analyses of human conduct. In this discipline, decision making is regarded as the central task of management and is characterized as a process of information gathering and processing. Rational behavior is seen as a consequence of choosing among alternatives according to an evaluation of outcomes. Simon characterizes the basic assumption of decision-making theory as follows:

> At each moment the behaving subject, or the organization composed of numbers of such individuals, is confronted with a large number of alternative behaviors, some of which are present in consciousness and some of which are not. Decision, or choice, as the term is used here, is the process by which one of these alternatives for each moment's behavior is selected to be carried out. The series of such decisions which determines behavior over some stretch of time may be called a *strategy....* If any one of the possible strategies is chosen and followed out, certain consequences will result. The task of rational decision is to select that one of the strategies which is followed by the preferred set of consequences. — Simon, *Administrative Behavior* (1976), p. 67.

Simon asserts that *rational* decision making is a process of choosing among alternatives, and that it involves a series of steps:

1. Listing all the alternative strategies.

2. Determining all the consequences that follow upon each of these strategies.

3. Comparatively evaluating these sets of consequences.

In the literature on computers and decision making, a wide range of human activities and concerns are subjected to this kind of analysis. Researchers in simulation, operations research, and game theory (all within what Boguslaw, in *The New Utopians* (1965), calls the 'formalist approach') apply sophisticated mathematical methods to decisions as varied as the routing of telephone calls, the choice of advertising media for a new product, and the selection of targets for bombing.

These techniques are based on the development of a formal model for the system that will be affected, a set of rules that describe the behavior of the modelled system, and an objective means of assigning valuations to the resulting effects. When calculations based on the model, rules, and valuations are performed, alternatives can be compared and the most highly valued (optimal) one selected.

There have been critiques of this idealization, often from people within management science who object to the narrow assumptions of the formalist approach. Simon, for example, continues his description of the assumptions given above, noting that:

> ... The word 'all' is used advisedly. It is obviously impossible for the individual to know 'all' his alternatives or 'all' their consequences, and this impossibility is a very important departure of actual behavior from the model of objective rationality. — Simon, *Administrative Behavior*, p. 67.

This caveat is the major contribution of Simon. He treats objective rationality as an idealization, rarely (if ever) achieved in a real situation. Practical decision making only roughly approximates this ideal:

> It is impossible for the behavior of a single, isolated individual to reach any high degree of rationality. The number of alternatives he must explore is so great, the information he would need to evaluate them so vast that even an approximation of objective rationality is hard to conceive.... Actual behavior falls short, in at least three ways, of objective rationality as defined in the last chapter:
>
> 1. Rationality requires a complete knowledge and anticipation of the consequences that will follow on each choice. In fact, knowledge of consequences is always fragmentary.
>
> 2. Since these consequences lie in the future, imagination must supply the lack of experienced feeling in attaching value to them. But values can be only imperfectly anticipated.
>
> 3. Rationality requires a choice among all possible alternative behaviors. In actual behavior, only a very few of all these possible alternatives ever come to mind. — Simon, *Administrative Behavior*, pp. 79ff.

It is important to note, however, that this critique is not an objection to the rationalistic approach, but to the assumption of *full* knowledge and rationality in applying optimization techniques. Simon argues that systematic reasoning rules can be applied for effective decision making, and can be programmed into computers. Rather than computing all of the consequences, the computer must operate with 'bounded rationality.'

Simon's decision-making theories developed into more general theories of 'problem solving' as he and others made the first attempts to build intelligent computer programs. Rather than concentrating on the kinds of decisions that managers make, researchers studied tasks (such as proving logic theorems and solving simple puzzles) that could be viewed as problems of search in a space of alternatives. The task is characterized in terms of a 'problem space.' Each 'node' of the space is reached by some sequence of actions, and has some consequences relevant to structure of the task. The computer program searches for a solution in this potentially huge space of possibilities, using 'heuristics' to guide the search and to provide valuations. In this search it will explore only some of the possible alternatives, and will apply its valuation heuristics in the absence of full knowledge.

Programs of this sort are described more fully in Chapter 8, and are the textbook examples of artificial intelligence. There is a widely accepted definition of what constitutes 'general problem-solving behavior:'

> A person is confronted with a *problem* when he wants something and does not know immediately what series of actions he can perform to get it.... To have a problem implies (at least) that certain information is given to the problem solver: information about what is desired, under what conditions, by means of what tools and operations, starting with what initial information, and with access to what resources. The problem solver has an interpretation of this information—exactly that interpretation which lets us label some part of it as *goal*, another part as *side conditions*, and so on. Consequently, if we provide a representation for this information (in symbol structures), and assume that the interpretation of these structures is implicit in the program of the problem solving IPS [Information Processing System], then we have defined a problem.
> — Newell and Simon, *Human Problem Solving* (1972), pp. 72-73.

There are several key elements to this view of problem solving, which is generally taken for granted in artificial intelligence research:

1. **Task environment.** First, we characterize the problem in terms of a 'task environment' in which there are different potential 'states' of

affairs, 'actions' available to the problem solver to change the state, and 'goals' from which rational actions can be derived.

2. **Internal representation.** Second, the problem solver has some kind of 'representation' of the task environment. This representation is a collection of 'symbol structures' that are part of the constitution of the problem solver. They correspond in a systematic way to the task environment.

3. **Search.** The problem solver goes through an information process that can be analyzed as a search among alternative courses of action, in order to find those that will lead to a desired goal.

4. **Choice.** Finally, a rational agent will select the course of action among those found that best achieves the desired goals. Newell, in "The knowledge level" (1982, p. 102), calls this the 'principle of rationality': "If an agent has knowledge that one of its actions will lead to one of its goals, then the agent will select that action." Of course we must allow for the case in which more than one action may lead to one of the goals, so we cannot predict the specific action, but just that "The action that occurs at any instant is a member of the selected set of actions."

More formally, we can describe the operation of the problem solver in terms of a search in a problem space determined by the task environment and internal representation. Although there is much to be said about just how this can be applied to different cases (for example, the role played by having multiple representations, as discussed by Bobrow in "Dimensions of representation," 1975), the differences are not germane to answering our larger questions about what computers can do. There is a shared background that cuts across the detailed schools of artificial intelligence and that is in general accord with the rationalistic tradition. We will explore some of these topics more fully in Chapter 11.

2.4 Cognitive science

In recent years there have been efforts to unify theories of human thought and language from within the rationalistic tradition under a new discipline known as 'cognitive science.' Initially, several books were put forth as volumes in cognitive science.[6] The journal *Cognitive Science* began

---

[6]Bobrow and Collins's *Representation and Understanding* (1975), Schank and Abelson's *Scripts Plans Goals and Understanding* (1977), and Norman and Rumelhart's *Explorations in Cognition* (1975) were among the first.

publication in 1977, and the Cognitive Science Society held its first annual meeting in 1979.[7] A number of other conferences, journals, and research funding programs have followed.

Of course cognitive science is not really new. It deals with phenomena of thought and language that have occupied philosophers and scientists for thousands of years. Its boundaries are vague, but it is clear that much of linguistics, psychology, artificial intelligence, and the philosophy of mind fall within its scope. In declaring that it exists as a science, people are marking the emergence of what Lakatos calls a 'research programme.'[8] Lakatos chooses this term in preference to Kuhn's 'paradigm' (*The Structure of Scientific Revolutions*, 1962) to emphasize the active role that a research programme plays in guiding the activity of scientists. He sees the history of science not as a cyclic pattern of revolution and normal science, but as a history of competing research programmes. He distinguishes between 'mature science,' consisting of research programmes, and 'immature science,' consisting of "a mere patched up pattern of trial and error."

A research programme is more than a set of specific plans for carrying out scientific activities. The observable details of the programme reflect a deeper coherence which is not routinely examined. In the day-to-day business of research, writing, and teaching, scientists operate within a background of belief about how things are. This background invisibly shapes what they choose to do and how they choose to do it. A research programme grows up within a tradition of thought. It is the result of many influences, some recognized explicitly and others concealed in the social structure and language of the community. Efforts to understand and modify the research programme are made within that same context, and can never escape it to produce an 'objective' or 'correct' approach.

The research programme of cognitive science encompasses work that has been done under different disciplinary labels, but is all closely related through its roots in the rationalistic tradition. Cognitive science needs to be distinguished from 'cognitive psychology,' which is the branch of traditional (experimental) psychology dealing with cognition. Although cognitive psychology constitutes a substantial part of what is seen as cognitive science, it follows specific methodological principles that limit its scope. In particular, it is based on an experimental approach in which progress is made by performing experiments that can directly judge between competing scientific hypotheses about the nature of cognitive mech-

---

[7]Norman, *Perspectives on Cognitive Science* (1981), is a collection of presentations from that conference. They were intended to define the science and explain its significance.

[8]See Lakatos, "Falsification and the methodology of scientific research programmes" (1970). In order to avoid confusion in our discussion of computers and computer programs, we will consistently follow Lakatos's use of the British spelling, 'programme,' when using the word in this sense.

anisms. In most experiments, situations are created in which the variety of action is strictly controlled and only a very limited aspect of the situation is considered relevant to the patterns of recurrence (typical examples are experiments with rats in mazes, nonsense-syllable memorization, and the matching of geometrical figures to simple descriptions).

The assumption underlying this empirical research is that general laws can be found in these restricted cases that will apply (albeit in a more complex way) to a much broader spectrum of cognitive activity. It is also implicitly assumed that these laws will have the same general form as those of sciences like physics, and can be subjected to rigid experimental test.

In the last few decades, simple forms of cognitive psychology have been challenged by advocates of 'information-processing psychology,' who assert that cognitive systems can be best understood by analogy to programmed computers. The assumptions behind this approach can be summarized as follows:

1. All cognitive systems are symbol systems. They achieve their intelligence by symbolizing external and internal situations and events, and by manipulating those symbols.

2. All cognitive systems share a basic underlying set of symbol manipulating processes.

3. A theory of cognition can be couched as a program in an appropriate symbolic formalism such that the program when run in the appropriate environment will produce the observed behavior.

This approach is not incompatible with the earlier non-computational models. In general the rules postulated as governing recurrences could be embedded in appropriate programs. In this sense, a program is a formal system that has some number of variables and that can be manipulated (run) to generate predictions about the behavior (outputs) of some naturally occurring system that it is intended to model. To the extent that the predicted behavior corresponds to that observed, the theory is supported. The role of the computer is to enable the scientist to deal with more complex theories than those whose consequences could be determined by examination or by manual computation. This makes it feasible for cognitive theories to be more intricate and complicated than their predecessors and still remain under empirical control.

In trying to deal with phenomena that do not have the obvious limitations of the sparse experimental situations of cognitive psychology, researchers have turned to artificial intelligence—the design and testing of computer programs that carry out activities patterned after human thought and language. These programs are then taken as theories of the corresponding human behavior. As Simon says in "Cognitive science: The newest science of the artificial" (1981, p. 24): "Most of our knowledge [of intelligence] will have to come from...observation of the vast variety of intelligent systems...and from formal theories—mainly in the form of computer programs—induced from that body of observation."

Many difficult issues are raised by the attempt to relate programs to theory and to cognitive mechanisms. Within the cognitive science community, there is much debate about just what role computer programs have in developing and testing theories. We will not present the details of that debate, however. It is more important to understand how the discourse is determined by a taken-for-granted background shaped by the underlying assumptions of the rationalistic tradition, as we have outlined in this chapter. In the rest of this book we pose challenges to those assumptions, and in the end argue that we need to replace the rationalistic orientation if we want to understand human thought, language, and action, or to design effective computer tools. Implicit in our critique is a statement about the cognitive science research programme—not that it is vacuous or useless, but that it will have important limitations in its scope and in its power to explain what we are and what we do.[9]

---

[9]For an excellent overview of both the history and current direction of cognitive science, see Gardner, *The Mind's New Science* (1985).

Chapter 3

Understanding and Being

In this chapter we introduce Heidegger's analysis of understanding and Being. Heidegger's writings are both important and difficult, and we will make no attempt to give a thorough or authoritative exposition. Our intention is to bring out those aspects relevant to our examination of language and thought and to our understanding of technology. Before turning to Heidegger, however, it will be useful to look briefly at issues that arise in interpreting texts. In addition to the obvious relevance of this material to our discussion of language, we have found that it is easier to grasp the more radical phenomenological statements about interpretation if we first consider interpretive activity in a more obvious setting.

When someone speaks of 'interpretation,' the most likely association is with artistic or literary works. The musician, the literary critic, and the ordinary reader of a poem or novel are all in some immediate sense 'interpreting' a collection of marks on a page. One of the fundamental insights of phenomenology is that this activity of interpretation is not limited to such situations, but pervades our everyday life. In coming to an understanding of what it means to think, understand, and act, we need to recognize the role of interpretation.

3.1 Hermeneutics

Hermeneutics[1] began as the theory of the interpretation of texts, particularly mythical and sacred texts. Its practitioners struggled with the problem of characterizing how people find meaning in a text that exists over many centuries and is understood differently in different epochs. A

---

[1] Palmer's *Hermeneutics* (1969) is an excellent first introduction to hermeneutics, including both its historical roots and its current meaning for literary criticism.

mythical or religious text continues to be spoken or read and to serve as a source of deep meaning, in spite of changes in the underlying culture and even in the language. There are obvious questions to be raised. Is the meaning definable in some absolute sense, independent of the context in which the text was written? Is it definable only in terms of that original context? If so, is it possible or desirable for a reader to transcend his or her own culture and the intervening history in order to recover the correct interpretation?

If we reject the notion that the meaning is in the text, are we reduced to saying only that a particular person at a particular moment had a particular interpretation? If so, have we given up a naive but solid-seeming view of the reality of the meaning of the text in favor of a relativistic appeal to individual subjective reaction?

Within hermeneutics there has been an ongoing debate between those who place the meaning within the text and those who see meaning as grounded in a process of understanding in which the text, its production, and its interpretation all play a vital part. As we will show in Chapter 5, this debate has close parallels with current issues in linguistic and semantic theory.

For the objectivist school of hermeneutics,[2] the text must have a meaning that exists independently of the act of interpretation. The goal of a hermeneutic theory (a theory of interpretation) is to develop methods by which we rid ourselves of all prejudices and produce an objective analysis of what is really there. The ideal is to completely 'decontextualize' the text.

The opposing approach, most clearly formulated by Gadamer,[3] takes the act of interpretation as primary, understanding it as an interaction between the *horizon*[4] provided by the text and the horizon that the interpreter brings to it. Gadamer insists that every reading or hearing of a text constitutes an act of giving meaning to it through interpretation.

Gadamer devotes extensive discussion to the relation of the individual to tradition, clarifying how tradition and interpretation interact. Any individual, in understanding his or her world, is continually involved in activities of interpretation. That interpretation is based on prejudice (or *pre-understanding*), which includes assumptions implicit in the language

---

[2]Emilio Betti (*Teoria Generale della Interpretazione*, 1955) has been the most influential supporter of this approach. Hirsch's *Validity in Interpretation* (1967) applies Betti's view to problems of literary criticism.

[3]Gadamer, *Truth and Method* (1975) and *Philosophical Hermeneutics* (1976).

[4]In his discussions of hermeneutics, Gadamer makes frequent reference to a person's 'horizon.' As with many of the words we will introduce in this chapter, there is no simple translation into previously understood terms. The rest of the chapter will serve to elucidate its meaning through its use.

that the person uses.[5] That language in turn is learned through activities
of interpretation. The individual is changed through the use of language,
and the language changes through its use by individuals. This process is
of the first importance, since it constitutes the background of the beliefs
and assumptions that determine the nature of our being.[6] We are social
creatures:

> In fact history does not belong to us, but we belong to it.
> Long before we understand ourselves through the process of
> self-examination, we understand ourselves in a self-evident way
> in the family, society and state in which we live. The focus of
> subjectivity is a distorting mirror. The self-awareness of the
> individual is only a flickering in the closed circuits of historical
> life. That is why the prejudices of the individual, far more than
> his judgments, constitute the historical reality of his being. —
> Gadamer, *Truth and Method* (1975), p. 245.

Gadamer sees in this essential historicity of our being the cause of our
inability to achieve full explicit understanding of ourselves. The nature of
our being is determined by our cultural background, and since it is formed
in our very way of experiencing and living in language, it cannot be made
fully explicit in that language:

> To acquire an awareness of a situation is, however, always a
> task of particular difficulty. The very idea of a situation means
> that we are not standing outside it and hence are unable to
> have any objective knowledge of it. We are always within the
> situation, and to throw light on it is a task that is never en-
> tirely completed. This is true also of the hermeneutic situation,
> i.e., the situation in which we find ourselves with regard to the
> tradition that we are trying to understand. The illumination
> of this situation—effective-historical reflection—can never be
> completely achieved, but this is not due to a lack in the re-
> flection, but lies in the essence of the historical being which is
> ours. To exist historically means that knowledge of oneself can
> never be complete. — Gadamer, *Truth and Method* (1975), pp.
> 268-269.

---

[5]The attempt to elucidate our own pre-understanding is the central focus of the
branch of sociology called 'ethnomethodology,' as exemplified by Garfinkel, "What
is ethnomethodology" (1967), Goffman, *The Presentation of Self in Everyday Life* (1959),
and Cicourel, *Cognitive Sociology* (1974).

[6]The widely mentioned 'Sapir-Whorf hypothesis' is a related but somewhat simpler
account, in that it emphasizes the importance of a language-determined 'world view'
without relating it to tradition and interpretation.

We can become aware of some of our prejudices, and in that way emancipate ourselves from some of the limits they place on our thinking. But we commit a fallacy in believing we can ever be free of all prejudice. Instead of striving for a means of getting away from our own pre-understanding, a theory of interpretation should aim at revealing the ways in which that pre-understanding interacts with the text.

Gadamer's approach accepts the inevitability of the *hermeneutic circle*. The meaning of an individual text is contextual, depending on the moment of interpretation and the horizon brought to it by the interpreter. But that horizon is itself the product of a history of interactions in language, interactions which themselves represent texts that had to be understood in the light of pre-understanding. What we understand is based on what we already know, and what we already know comes from being able to understand.

Gadamer's discourse on language and tradition is based on a rather broad analysis of interpretation and understanding. If we observe the hermeneutic circle only at the coarse-grained level offered by texts and societies, we remain blind to its operation at the much finer-grained level of daily life. If we look only at language, we fail to relate it to the interpretation that constitutes non-linguistic experience as well. It is therefore necessary to adopt a deeper approach in which interpretation is taken as relevant to ontology—to our understanding of what it means for something or someone to exist.

3.2 Understanding and ontology

Gadamer, and before him Heidegger, took the hermeneutic idea of interpretation beyond the domain of textual analysis, placing it at the very foundation of human cognition. Just as we can ask how interpretation plays a part in a person's interaction with a text, we can examine its role in our understanding of the world as a whole.

Heidegger and Gadamer reject the commonsense philosophy of our culture in a deep and fundamental way. The prevalent understanding is based on the metaphysical revolution of Galileo and Descartes, which grew out of a tradition going back to Plato and Aristotle. This understanding, which goes hand in hand with what we have called the 'rationalistic orientation,' includes a kind of mind-body dualism that accepts the existence of two separate domains of phenomena, the *objective* world of physical reality, and the *subjective* mental world of an individual's thoughts and feelings. Simply put, it rests on several taken-for-granted assumptions:

1. We are inhabitants of a 'real world' made up of objects bearing properties. Our actions take place in that world.

2. There are 'objective facts' about that world that do not depend on the interpretation (or even the presence) of any person.

3. Perception is a process by which facts about the world are (sometimes inaccurately) registered in our thoughts and feelings.

4. Thoughts and intentions about action can somehow cause physical (hence real-world) motion of our bodies.

Much of philosophy has been an attempt to understand how the mental and physical domains are related—how our perceptions and thoughts relate to the world toward which they are directed. Some schools have denied the existence of one or the other. Some argue that we cannot coherently talk about the mental domain, but must understand all behavior in terms of the physical world, which includes the physical structure of our bodies. Others espouse solipsism, denying that we can establish the existence of an objective world at all, since our own mental world is the only thing of which we have immediate knowledge. Kant called it "a scandal of philosophy and of human reason in general" that over the thousands of years of Western culture, no philosopher had been able to provide a sound argument refuting psychological idealism—to answer the question "How can I know whether anything outside of my subjective consciousness exists?"

Heidegger argues that "the 'scandal of philosophy' is not that this proof has yet to be given, but that *such proofs are expected and attempted again and again.*"[7] He says of Kant's "Refutation of Idealism" that it shows "...how intricate these questions are and how what one wants to prove gets muddled with what one does prove and with the means whereby the proof is carried out."[8] Heidegger's work grew out of the questions of *phenomenology* posed by his teacher Husserl, and developed into a quest for an understanding of *Being*. He argues that the separation of subject and object denies the more fundamental unity of *being-in-the-world (Dasein)*. By drawing a distinction that I (the subject) am perceiving something else (the object), I have stepped back from the primacy of experience and understanding that operates without reflection.

Heidegger rejects both the simple objective stance (the objective physical world is the primary reality) and the simple subjective stance (my thoughts and feelings are the primary reality), arguing instead that it is impossible for one to exist without the other. The interpreted and the interpreter do not exist independently: existence is interpretation, and interpretation is existence. Prejudice is not a condition in which the subject

---

[7]Heidegger, *Being and Time* (1962), p. 249, emphasis in original.

[8]Ibid., p. 247.

is led to interpret the world falsely, but is the necessary condition of having a background for interpretation (hence Being). This is clearly expressed in the later writings of Gadamer:

> It is not so much our judgments as it is our prejudices that constitute our being.... the historicity of our existence entails that prejudices, in the literal sense of the word, constitute the initial directedness of our whole ability to experience. Prejudices are biases of our openness to the world. They are simply conditions whereby we experience something—whereby what we encounter says something to us. — Gadamer, *Philosophical Hermeneutics* (1976), p. 9.

We cannot present here a thorough discussion of Heidegger's philosophy, but will outline some points that are relevant to our later discussion:[9]

Our implicit beliefs and assumptions cannot all be made explicit. Heidegger argues that the practices in terms of which we render the world and our own lives intelligible cannot be made exhaustively explicit. There is no neutral viewpoint from which we can see our beliefs as things, since we always operate within the framework they provide. This is the essential insight of the hermeneutic circle, applied to understanding as a whole.

The inevitability of this circularity does not negate the importance of trying to gain greater understanding of our own assumptions so that we can expand our horizon. But it does preclude the possibility that such understanding will ever be objective or complete. As Heidegger says in *Being and Time* (1962, p. 194), "But if we see this circle as a vicious one and look out for ways of avoiding it, even if we just sense it as an inevitable imperfection, then the art of understanding has been misunderstood from the ground up."

Practical understanding is more fundamental than detached theoretical understanding. The Western philosophical tradition is based on the assumption that the detached theoretical point of view is superior to the involved practical viewpoint. The scientist or philosopher who devises theories is discovering how things really are, while in everyday life we have only a clouded idea. Heidegger reverses this, insisting that we have primary access to the world through practical involvement with the *ready-to-hand*—the world in which we are always acting unreflectively. Detached contemplation can be illuminating, but it also obscures the phenomena

---

[9]This overview is based on Dreyfus's *Being-in-the-World: A Commentary on Division I of Heidegger's Being and Time* (in press). It uses some of his discussion directly, but also includes our own interpretations for which he cannot be held responsible.

themselves by isolating and categorizing them. Much of the current study of logic, language, and thought gives primacy to activities of detached contemplation. Heidegger does not disregard this kind of thinking, but puts it into a context of cognition as *praxis*—as concernful acting in the world. He is concerned with our condition of *thrownness*—the condition of understanding in which our actions find some resonance or effectiveness in the world.

We do not relate to things primarily through having representations of them. Connected to both of the preceding points is Heidegger's rejection of *mental representations.* The common sense of our tradition is that in order to perceive and relate to things, we must have some content in our minds that corresponds to our knowledge of them. If we focus on concernful activity instead of on detached contemplation, the status of this representation is called into question. In driving a nail with a hammer (as opposed to thinking about a hammer), I need not make use of any explicit representation of the hammer. My ability to act comes from my familiarity with *hammering*, not my knowledge of *a hammer.* This skepticism concerning mental representations is in strong opposition to current approaches in cognitive psychology, linguistics, artificial intelligence, and the foundation of cognitive science, as described in Chapter 2. Representation is so taken for granted that it is hard to imagine what would be left if it were abandoned. One of the major issues discussed in later chapters is the connection between representation and mechanism; this discussion will aid our understanding of what it means to take seriously Heidegger's questioning of mental representation.

Meaning is fundamentally social and cannot be reduced to the meaning-giving activity of individual subjects. The rationalistic view of cognition is individual-centered. We look at language by studying the characteristics of an individual language learner or language user, and at reasoning by describing the activity of an individual's deduction process. Heidegger argues that this is an inappropriate starting point—that we must take social activity as the ultimate foundation of intelligibility, and even of existence. A person is not an individual subject or ego, but a manifestation of *Dasein* within a space of possibilities, situated within a world and within a tradition.

3.3 An illustration of thrownness

Many people encountering the work of Heidegger for the first time find it very difficult to comprehend. Abstract terms like 'Dasein' and 'thrownness,' for instance, are hard to relate to reality. This is the opposite of what Heidegger intends. His philosophy is based on a deep awareness of everyday life. He argues that the issues he discusses are difficult not because they are abstruse, but because they are concealed by their 'ordinary everydayness.'

In order to give more of a sense of the importance of thrownness (which will play a large role in the second half of the book), it may be useful to consider a simple example that evokes experiences of thrownness for many readers.

Imagine that you are chairing a meeting of fifteen or so people, at which some important and controversial issue is to be decided: say, the decision to bring a new computer system into the organization. As the meeting goes on you must keep things going in a productive direction, deciding whom to call on, when to cut a speaker off, when to call for an end of discussion or a vote, and so forth. There are forcefully expressed differences of opinion, and if you don't take a strong role the discussion will quickly deteriorate into a shouting match dominated by the loudest, who will keep repeating their own fixed positions in hopes of wearing everyone else down.

We can make a number of observations about your situation:

You cannot avoid acting. At every moment, you are in a position of authority, and your actions affect the situation. If you just sit there for a time, letting things go on in the direction they are going, that in itself constitutes an action, with effects that you may or may not want. You are 'thrown' into action independent of your will.

You cannot step back and reflect on your actions. Anyone who has been in this kind of situation has afterwards felt "I should have said..." or "I shouldn't have let Joe get away with..." In the need to respond immediately to what people say and do, it is impossible to take time to analyze things explicitly and choose the best course of action. In fact, if you stop to do so you will miss some of what is going on, and implicitly choose to let it go on without interruption. You are thrown on what people loosely call your 'instincts,' dealing with whatever comes up.

The effects of actions cannot be predicted. Even if you had time to reflect, it is impossible to know how your actions will affect other people. If you decide to cut someone off in order to get to another topic, the group may object to your heavy-handedness, that in itself becoming a topic of discussion. If you avoid calling on someone whose opinion you don't like, you may find that he shouts it out, or that a friend feels compelled to take up his point of view. Of course this doesn't imply that things are total chaos, but simply that you cannot count on careful rational planning to find steps that will achieve your goals. You must, as the idiom goes, 'flow with the situation.'

You do not have a stable representation of the situation. In the post-mortem analysis, you will observe that there were significant patterns. "There were two factions, with the Smith group trying to oppose the computer via the strategy of keeping the discussion on costs and away from an analysis of what we are doing now, and the Wilson group trying to be sure that whether or not we got the computer, they would remain in control of the scheduling policies. Evans was the key, since he could go either way, and they brought up the training issue because that is his bailiwick and they knew he wouldn't want the extra headaches." In a sense you have a representation of the situation, with objects (e.g., the two factions) and properties (their goals, Evans's lack of prior loyalty, etc.), but this was not the understanding you had to work with as it was developing. Pieces of it may have emerged as the meeting went on, but they were fragmentary, possibly contradictory, and may have been rejected for others as things continued.

Every representation is an interpretation. Even in the post-mortem, your description of what was going on is hardly an objective analysis of the kind that could be subjected to proof. Two people at the same meeting could well come away with very different interpretations. Evans might say "Smith is competing with me for that promotion, and he wanted to bring up the training issue to point out that we've been having difficulty in our group lately." There is no ultimate way to determine that any one interpretation is really right or wrong, and even the people whose behavior is in question may well not be in touch with their own deep motivations.

Language is action. Each time you speak you are doing something quite different from simply 'stating a fact.' If you say "First we have to address the issue of system development" or "Let's have somebody on the other side talk," you are not describing the situation but creating it. The existence of "the issue of system development" or "the other side" is an interpretation, and in mentioning it you bring your interpretation into the group discourse. Of course others can object "That isn't really an issue—you're confusing two things" or "We aren't taking sides, everyone has his own opinion." But whether or not your characterization is taken for granted or taken as the basis for argument, you have created the objects and properties it describes by virtue of making the utterance.

Heidegger recognized that ordinary everyday life is like the situation we have been describing. Our interactions with other people and with the

inanimate world we inhabit put us into a situation of thrownness, for which
the metaphor of the meeting is much more apt than the metaphor of the
objective detached scientist who makes observations, forms hypotheses,
and consciously chooses a rational course of action.

3.4   Breaking down and readiness-to-hand

Another aspect of Heidegger's thought that is difficult for many people
to assimilate to their previous understanding is his insistence that objects
and properties are not inherent in the world, but arise only in an event of
breaking down in which they become *present-at-hand*. One simple example
he gives is that of a hammer being used by someone engaged in driving a
nail. To the person doing the hammering, the hammer as such does not
exist. It is a part of the background of *readiness-to-hand* that is taken for
granted without explicit recognition or identification as an object. It is
part of the hammerer's world, but is not present any more than are the
tendons of the hammerer's arm.

The hammer presents itself as a hammer only when there is some kind
of breaking down or *unreadiness-to-hand*. Its 'hammerness' emerges if
it breaks or slips from grasp or mars the wood, or if there is a nail to
be driven and the hammer cannot be found. The point is a subtle one,
closely related to the distinction between thrownness and reflection on
one's actions, as discussed above. As observers, we may talk about the
hammer and reflect on its properties, but for the person engaged in the
thrownness of unhampered hammering, it does not exist as an entity.

Some other examples may help convey the importance of this distinction. As I watch my year-old baby learn to walk and pick up objects, I
may be tempted to say that she is 'learning about gravity.' But if I really
want to deal with her ontology—with the world as it exists for her—there
is no such thing as gravity. It would be inappropriate to view her learning
as having anything to do with a concept or representation of gravity and
its effects, even though she is clearly learning the skills that are necessary
for acting in a physical world that we (as adult observers) characterize in
terms of abstractions like 'gravity.' For the designer of space vehicles, on
the other hand, it is clear that gravity exists. In anticipating the forms
of breaking down that will occur when the normal background of gravity
is altered, the designer must deal with gravity as a phenomenon to be
considered, represented, and manipulated.

If we turn to computer systems, we see that for different people, engaged in different activities, the existence of objects and properties emerges
in different kinds of breaking down. As I sit here typing a draft on a word
processor, I am in the same situation as the hammerer. I think of words

and they appear on my screen. There is a network of equipment that includes my arms and hands, a keyboard, and many complex devices that mediate between it and a screen. None of this equipment is present for me except when there is a breaking down. If a letter fails to appear on the screen, the keyboard may emerge with properties such as 'stuck keys.' Or I may discover that the program was in fact constructed from separate components such as a 'screen manager' and a 'keyboard handler,' and that certain kinds of 'bugs' can be attributed to the keyboard handler. If the problem is serious, I may be called upon to bring forth a complex network of properties reflecting the design of the system and the details of computer software and hardware.

For me, the writer, this network of objects and properties did not exist previously. The typing was part of my world, but not the structure that emerges as I try to cope with the breakdown. But of course it did exist for someone else—for the people who created the device by a process of conscious design. They too, though, took for granted a background of equipment which, in the face of breaking down, they could have further brought to light.

In sum, Heidegger insists that it is meaningless to talk about the existence of objects and their properties in the absence of concernful activity, with its potential for breaking down. What really *is* is not defined by an objective omniscient observer, nor is it defined by an individual—the writer or computer designer—but rather by a space of potential for human concern and action. In the second part of the book we will show how shifting from a rationalistic to a Heideggerian perspective can radically alter our conception of computers and our approach to computer design.

Chapter 4

Cognition as a biological phenomenon

The previous chapter presented the primary basis for our theoretical orientation, but our own understanding initially developed through a different path. The rationalistic orientation of our prior training in science and technology made the foundations of hermeneutics and phenomenology nearly inaccessible to us. Before we could become open to their relevance and importance we needed to take a preliminary step towards unconcealing the tradition in which we lived, recognizing that it was in fact open to serious question.

For us, this first step came through the work of Humberto Maturana, a biologist who has been concerned with understanding how biological processes can give rise to the phenomena of cognition and language. Beginning with a study of the neurophysiology of vision, which led to the classic work on the functional organization of the frog's retina,[1] he went on to develop a theory of the organization of living systems[2] and of language and cognition.[3]

---

[1] Maturana et al., "Anatomy and physiology of vision in the frog" (1960).

[2] Maturana, "The organization of the living: A theory of the living organization" (1975); Maturana and Varela, *Autopoiesis and Cognition* (1980).

[3] See, for example, Maturana, "Neurophysiology of cognition" (1970), "Cognitive strategies" (1974), "Biology of language: The epistemology of reality" (1978). Much of Maturana's theory was developed in conjunction with Francisco Varela, whose own work is further developed in Varela, *Principles of Biological Autonomy* (1979), "Living ways of sense making: A middle way approach to neurosciences" (1984), and *El Arbol de Conocimiento* (forthcoming). Maturana was deeply influenced by work in cybernetics by von Foerster and others in the Biological Computer Laboratory at the University of Illinois. The book *Cybernetics of Cybernetics* (von Foerster, 1974),

In comparing Maturana's orientation to Heidegger's, it is important to recognize that they began in very different traditions. As we mentioned in the previous chapter, there is a long history within philosophy of viewing mental and physical descriptions as applying in incommensurate domains. In approaches based on this 'dualism' it is taken for granted that mental predications (such as "X knows that Y" or "X perceives a Y") are not expressible in terms of physical descriptions of a nervous system. Having made this assumption, it becomes a confusion of levels to ask whether a particular physical activity of the nervous system is a 'perception' or whether a certain state is one in which the organism 'knows' some 'fact.'

Among the scientists who work in areas such as neurophysiology and artificial intelligence, however, it is a strongly held working hypothesis that there is a systematic and recurrent relationship between the two domains. It is assumed that "X sees a red spot" can be correlated with a particular pattern of activity in the retina and visual cortex, or that "John believes that Brutus killed Caesar" can be associated with a particular pattern of data in John's brain, viewed as a computer with appropriate software and storage devices. Few researchers adopt the naive approach of looking for immediate correlations between the mental and the physical except in peripheral functions like the image manipulation done by the retina. Usually the argument is based on an analogy to computer programs, in which the organization of the software provides a level of 'functional description' that is abstracted away from the specifics of the physical implementation. An entity counts as being explained when its behavior can be described in terms of a compositional analysis that postulates parts that are functionally identified—that play functionally defined roles in its operation.

It is possible to adopt the position, as Chomsky at times does,[4] that theories of cognition can deal purely with 'competence,' characterizing the behavior of the cognitive system while making no hypothesis concerning the generation of that behavior by mechanisms. Most cognitive scientists, however, find this stance too restrictive. As scientists, they take it for granted that all observable phenomena are ultimately explainable in terms of mechanistic systems operating according to regular laws. A cognitive theory needs to deal with the causal principles by which these systems operate, not just with abstract characterizations of the behavior they generate. The appropriate level of description for the causal regularities may be an abstract level of software, rather than the physical descriptions of individual components, but nevertheless it has the goal of explaining *why*

---

produced in that laboratory, provides a broad insight into its work. Since we have been most directly influenced by Maturana's writings we will refer primarily to them and to him.

[4]See, for example, Chomsky, *Reflections on Language* (1975).

things happen, not just characterizing what happens.

In creating such an explanation, it has generally been taken for granted that the distinctions and relations that are applied in describing the mental domain will form a basis for examining the structures in the domain of causal mechanism. Maturana, beginning as an experimental neurophysiologist, came to realize that this naive formulation was inadequate and that it obscured the phenomena he wanted to study. However, he also wanted to adhere to the scientific tradition of explanation in terms of deterministic physical systems, asking how such systems might give rise to cognitive phenomena.[5] Much of his writing, therefore, is directed toward revealing the pervasiveness of the pre-understanding that biologists and cognitive scientists bring to bear, and toward opening possibilities for a different understanding.

In his writings, Maturana introduces a good deal of new terminology which seems puzzling and difficult on first reading. He does this quite consciously, because he recognizes that the old terminology carries within it a pre-understanding that is a trap for new understanding. For example, in describing their use of the word 'autopoiesis' Maturana and Varela say:

> Curiously, but not surprisingly, the introduction of this word proved of great value. It simplified enormously the task of talking about the organization of the living without falling into the always gaping trap of not saying anything new because the language does not permit it. We could not escape being immersed in a tradition, but with an adequate language we could orient ourselves differently and, perhaps, from the new perspective generate a new tradition. — Maturana and Varela, *Autopoiesis and Cognition* (1980), p. xvii.

We introduce much of Maturana's terminology, without attempting to give definitions (indeed our own theory of language denies the possibility of giving precise definitions). The network of meanings will gradually evolve as the different ideas are developed and the links of their interdependence laid out. We cannot in these few pages give a complete or balanced account of Maturana's work. We have chosen instead to emphasize those aspects that were most critical in the development of our own understanding, trusting that for many readers this introduction will motivate the challenging but rewarding task of reading the original sources.

---

[5] As will become obvious in this chapter and throughout the book, the words 'cognitive' and 'cognition' are used in quite different ways by different writers. We will not attempt to give a simple definition of Maturana's use, but will clarify it through the discussion in the chapter.

4.1   The closure of the nervous system

In neurophysiological studies of vision, the traditional assumption (based on a rationalistic philosophy of cognition) was that the activity in the optic nerve was a direct representation of the pattern of light on the retina. The work of Maturana, Lettvin, McCulloch, and Pitts on "Anatomy and physiology of vision in the frog" (1960) challenged this, demonstrating that over large areas of the retina to which single fibers of the optic nerve were connected, it was not the light intensity itself but rather the pattern of local variation of intensity that excited the fiber. There was, for example, one type of fiber that responded best to a small dark spot surrounded by light. When triggered, it led to activity appropriate for catching a fly in the location corresponding to the spot. It became apparent that at least some of the cognitive processes that we would interpret as relevant to the survival of the frog actually take place within its visual system, not deeper in its neuroanatomy.

In trying to extend this research to color vision, Maturana, Uribe, and Frenk ("A biological theory of relativistic color coding in the primate retina," 1968) made observations that led to further questioning the relation between perception and the world being perceived. Making use of a simple observation that had been noted for many years, they argued that theories associating colors directly with wavelengths on the spectrum were inadequate. When a stick is illuminated by a white light from one side and a red light from the other, it casts two shadows, one of which appears red (against a generally pink background) and the other of which appears *green*. If we ask about the objective 'thing' being observed, there is no light with a spectrum of wavelengths normally called green; only various shades of red, white, and pink. However, Maturana and other researchers have postulated that the patterns of neural activity produced are the same as those produced by light of a single wavelength normally called green.[6] The presence of 'green' for the nervous system is not a simple correlate of the presence of certain wavelengths of light, but the result of a complex pattern of relative activity among different neurons.

This example was one of many that led Maturana to question the validity of our commonsense understanding of perception. On the naive view, there is some objectively recognizable property of a thing in the environment, and our perception of it is a capturing of that property in our mind. This idea is contained in the very words used in description:

> When Jerry Y. Lettvin and I wrote our several articles on frog vision..., we did it with the implicit assumption that we were

---

[6]The original work in this area is described in Land, "The retinex theory of color vision" (1977).

handling a clearly defined cognitive situation: there was an
objective (absolute) reality, external to the animal, and independent of it (not determined by it), which it could perceive
(cognize), and the animal could use the information obtained in
its perception to compute a behavior adequate to the perceived
situation. This assumption of ours appeared clearly in our language. We described the various kinds of retinal ganglion cells
as feature detectors, and we spoke about the detection of prey
and enemy. — Maturana, "Biology of cognition" (1970), p. xii.

Further examination of visual phenomena, however, suggested a different orientation. In order to deal with the seemingly fundamental per-
ceptual category of color it was necessary to give explanations in terms of
relative patterns of activity within the nervous system.

I soon realized in my research that my central purpose in the
study of color vision could not be the study of a mapping of
a colorful world on the nervous system, but rather that it had
to be the understanding of the participation of the retina (or
nervous system) in the generation of the color space of the
observer. — Maturana, "Biology of cognition" (1970), p. xii.

Perception, in other words, must be studied from the inside rather
than the outside—looking at the properties of the nervous system as a
generator of phenomena, rather than as a filter on the mapping of reality.

Maturana describes the nervous system as a closed network of interacting neurons such that any change in the state of relative activity of a
collection of neurons leads to a change in the state of relative activity of
other or the same collection of neurons. From this standpoint, the nervous system does not have 'inputs' and 'outputs.' It can be *perturbed* by
structural changes in the network itself, and this will affect its activity, but
the sequence of states of the system is generated by relations of neuronal
activity, as determined by its structure.

When light strikes the retina, it alters the structure of the nervous system by triggering chemical changes in the neurons. This changed structure
will lead to patterns of activity different from those that would have been
generated without the change, but it is a misleading simplification to view
this change as a perception of the light. If we inject an irritant into a
nerve, it triggers a change in the patterns of activity, but one which we
would hesitate to call a 'perception' of the irritant. Maturana argues that
all activity of the nervous system is best understood in this way. The
focus should be on the interactions within the system as a whole, not on
the structure of perturbations. The perturbations do not determine what
happens in the nervous system, but merely trigger changes of state. It is

the structure of the perturbed system that determines, or better, *specifies* what structural configurations of the medium[7] can perturb it.

From this perspective, there is no difference between perception and hallucination. If the injected irritant creates a pattern of neural activity identical to that which would be produced by heat applied to the area served by the nerve, then there is no neurophysiological sense to the question of whether the heat was really 'perceived' or was a 'hallucination.' At first, this refusal to distinguish reality from hallucination may seem far-fetched, but if we think back to color vision it is more plausible. The question of whether the shadow in the stick experiment was 'really green' is meaningless once we give up the notion that the perception of green corresponds in a simple way to a pattern of physical stimuli. In giving a scientific explanation of the operation of the nervous system at the physical level, we need to explain how the structure of the system at any moment generates the pattern of activity. The physical means by which that structure is changed by interaction within the physical medium lie outside the domain of the nervous system itself.

Of course an observer of the nervous system within its medium can make statements about the nature of the perturbation and its effect on patterns of activity. For this observer it makes sense to distinguish the situation of an injected irritant from one of heat. But *from the standpoint of the nervous system* it is not a relevant, or even possible, distinction.

Along with this new understanding of perception, Maturana argues against what he calls the 'fallacy of instructive interaction.' 'Instructive interaction' is his term for the commonsense belief that in our interactions with our environment we acquire a direct representation of it—that properties of the medium are mapped onto (specify the states of) structures in the nervous system. He argues that because our interaction is always through the activity of the entire nervous system, the changes are not in the nature of a mapping. They are the results of patterns of activity which, although triggered by changes in the physical medium, are not representations of it. The correspondences between the structural changes and the pattern of events that caused them are historical, not structural. They cannot be explained as a kind of reference relation between neural structures and an external world.

The structure of the organism at any moment determines a *domain of perturbations*—a space of possible effects the medium could have on the sequence of structural states that it could follow. The medium selects among these patterns, but does not generate the set of possibilities. In

---

[7]Here and throughout this chapter we use the term 'medium' rather than 'environment' to refer to the space in which an organism exists. This is to avoid the connotation that there is a separation between an entity and its 'environment.' An entity exists as part of a medium, not as a separate object inside it.

understanding an organism as a structure-determined system we view it in terms of its components and the interactions among them. The appropriate domain of description is not the behavior of the organism as a unity, but the interlocking behaviors of its physical components.

4.2 Autopoiesis, evolution, and learning

Maturana's understanding of an organism's relation to its environment leads to an epistemological problem. In our culture's commonsense theories of knowledge, what we know is a representation of the external world. Based on information gathered through perception, our brain somehow stores facts, uses them to draw conclusions, and updates them on the basis of experience.

If we look at the nervous system as closed, we must ask how an organism comes to have any knowledge of the world. How can a history of independent perturbations lead to the phenomena of cognition that our introspective intuitions will not let us deny? Maturana seeks to explain the origins of all phenomena of cognition in terms of the phylogeny (species history) and ontogeny (individual history) of living systems. To do this, he must first give an adequate account of the organization of the living. Maturana and Varela characterize the organization of the living as 'autopoietic.'[8] An autopoietic system is defined as:

> ... a network of processes of production (transformation and destruction) of components that produces the components that: (i) through their interactions and transformations continuously regenerate the network of processes (relations) that produced them; and (ii) constitute it (the machine) as a concrete unity in the space in which they (the components) exist by specifying the topological domain of its realization as such a network. —
> Maturana and Varela, *Autopoiesis and Cognition* (1980), p. 79.

The terms used in this definition, such as 'unity,' 'component,' and 'space,' have technical meanings in Maturana's work. We will not attempt to define them here, but will explicate their meaning in the course of describing the relevance of this definition.

The phenomenon of autopoiesis is quite general. It can apply to systems existing in any domain in which we can identify unities and components. An autopoietic system holds constant its organization and defines its boundaries through the continuous production of its components. If

---

[8]For a collection of papers by Maturana, Varela, and others on autopoiesis, see Zeleny, *Autopoiesis, a Theory of the Living Organization* (1978).

the autopoiesis is interrupted, the system's organization—its identity as a particular kind of unity—is lost, and the system disintegrates (dies). An autopoietic system that exists in physical space is a living system.[9]

At first sight, this definition may seem irrelevant or trivial. But it is in fact a carefully crafted statement expanding on a simple idea: the essential characteristic of a living system is that it is a collection of components constituting a unity that can live or die. Maturana's central observation is that exactly this simple property leads to the complex phenomena of life. The functioning of an organism as a structure-determined system with the potential of disintegration leads to adaptation and evolution.

The mechanism by which an organism comes to function adequately in its medium is one of selection, which includes both the selection of structural changes within an individual and the selection of individuals by the possibilities of survival and disintegration. A plastic, structure-determined system (i.e., one whose structure can change over time while its identity remains) that is autopoietic will by necessity evolve in such a way that its activities are properly coupled to its medium. Its structure must change so that it generates appropriate changes of state triggered by specific perturbing changes in its medium; otherwise it will disintegrate.

> Learning is not a process of accumulation of representations of the environment; it is a continuous process of transformation of behavior through continuous change in the capacity of the nervous system to synthesize it. Recall does not depend on the indefinite retention of a structural invariant that represents an entity (an idea, image, or symbol), but on the functional ability of the system to create, when certain recurrent conditions are given, a behavior that satisfies the recurrent demands or that the observer would class as a reenacting of a previous one. — Maturana, "Biology of cognition" (1970), p. 45.

Structural coupling is the basis not only for changes in an individual during its lifetime (learning) but also for changes carried through reproduction (evolution). In fact, all structural change can be viewed as ontogenetic (occurring in the life of an individual). A genetic mutation is a structural change to the parent which has no direct effect on its state of autopoiesis until it plays a role in the development of an offspring.

> If...the observer wants to discriminate between learned and instinctive behavior, he or she will discover that in their actual

---

[9] In later work, Maturana and Varela distinguish autopoiesis, as a property of cellular systems, from a more general property of *operational closure* that applies to a broader class of systems. We will not pursue the distinction here, but it is explicated in Varela's *El Arbol de Conocimiento* (forthcoming).

realization, both modes of behavior are equally determined in the present by the structures of the nervous system and organism, and that, in this respect, they are indeed indistinguishable. The distinction between learned and instinctive behaviors lies exclusively in the history of establishment of the structures responsible for them. — Maturana, "Biology of language" (1978), p. 45.

The structural coupling generated by the demands of autopoiesis plays the role that we naively attribute to having a representation of the world. The frog with optic fibers responding to small moving dark spots does not have a *representation* of flies. As a result of structural coupling, the structure of the nervous system generates patterns of activity that are triggered by specific perturbations and that contribute to the continued autopoiesis of the frog. Of course, the changes of structure that led to the frog's nervous system would not have been supportive of autopoiesis if the frog had to compete for food in a flyless environment. But it is an error to assume that the structure reflects a knowledge of the existence of flies. An explanation of why a frog catches a fly can be in two different domains. In the domain of the frog as a physical system we can explain how the structure determines the action. In the cognitive domain (discussed below), we can explain how the history of perturbations of the frog (and its ancestors) led to the structure that determines it.

4.3   The cognitive domain

Maturana's primary concern is to understand what 'cognition' can mean when we relate it to the fundamental nature of living systems. Rejecting the metaphor of information processing as the basis for cognition, he replaces the question "How does the organism obtain information about its environment?" with "How does it happen that the organism has the structure that permits it to operate adequately in the medium in which it exists?" An answer to this question cannot be generated by comprehending how a nervous system operates, but must be grounded in a deeper understanding of how cognitive activity is common to all life, and is determined by the underlying phenomenon of autopoiesis. As Maturana observes ("Neurophysiology of cognition," 1970, p. 8), "Living systems are cognitive systems, and living, as a process, is a process of cognition. This statement is valid for all organisms, with and without a nervous system."

What does it mean, then, to understand an organism as a cognitive system?

> A cognitive system is a system whose organization defines a domain of interactions in which it can act with relevance to the maintenance of itself, and the process of cognition is the actual (inductive) acting or behaving in this domain. — Maturana, "Biology of cognition" (1970), p. 13.

A cognitive explanation is one that deals with the *relevance* of action to the maintenance of autopoiesis. It operates in a *phenomenal domain* (domain of phenomena) that is distinct from the domain of mechanistic structure-determined behavior:

> ...as a result of the structural coupling that takes place along such a history, history becomes embodied both in the structure of the living system and the structure of the medium even though both systems necessarily, as structure determined systems, always operate in the present through locally determined processes.... History is necessary to explain how a given system or phenomenon came to be, but it does not participate in the explanation of the operation of the system or phenomenon in the present. — Maturana, "Biology of language" (1978), p. 39.

As observers we can generate descriptions of the activity of living systems in either of two non-intersecting domains. One description deals with the structure of the system and how that structure determines behavior. Such a description is essentially ahistorical. It does not matter how the system came to be that way, only that it is. We can at the same time describe (as observers of a history of changes within the structure and the medium) the pattern of interactions by which the structure came to be, and the relationship of those changes to effective action. It is this second domain of explanation that Maturana calls 'cognitive.' The cognitive domain deals with the relevance of the changing structure of the system to behavior that is effective for its survival.

It is therefore in this cognitive domain that we can make distinctions based on words such as 'intention,' 'knowledge,' and 'learning.' As mentioned above, philosophers have been careful to distinguish 'mental predicates' such as these from the physical predicates that apply to the organisms or machines embodying the phenomena they describe. For Maturana the cognitive domain is not simply a different (mental) level for providing a mechanistic description of the functioning of an organism. It is a domain for characterizing effective action through time. It is essentially temporal and historical. A statement like "The animal knows X" is not a statement about its state, but a statement about a pattern of actions (past and projected). One of Maturana's main objectives is to overcome the tendency (imposed on us by our language) to treat mental terms as though they could meaningfully be taken as descriptions of state or structure.

In making a distinction between the domain of cognition and the domain of the nervous system as a structure-determined system, Maturana clarifies an issue that has been at the heart of behaviorist approaches to cognition. The behaviorist describes the behavior of the organism (its responses) as a function of the sequence of states of the environment—the relevant stimuli, reinforcements, and punishments. In the most extreme form of behaviorism, it is assumed that stimuli and responses can be described externally without reference to the structure of the organism, and that all of the interesting recurrences of behavior can be explained by the patterning of the events. There are many who would call themselves behaviorists (or 'neobehaviorists'[10]) who postulate an internal state of an organism as well as the record of inputs and outputs. What is common to behaviorist approaches is the focus on the organism as a behaving entity (a unity, in Maturana's terms) subject to external stimuli, rather than as a composite to be understood through the interactions of its components.

Although he recognizes the significance of a domain that is independent of the structure of the cognitive system, Maturana rejects the behaviorist view, arguing that we cannot deal with 'organism' and 'environment' as two interacting independent things. We cannot identify stimuli that exist independently of the unity and talk about its history of responses to them. The unity itself specifies the space in which it exists, and in observing it we must use distinctions within that space.

4.4 Consensual domains

The sources of perturbation for an organism include other organisms of the same and different kinds. In the interaction between them, each organism undergoes a process of structural coupling due to the perturbations generated by the others. This mutual process can lead to interlocked patterns of behavior that form a *consensual domain*.

> When two or more organisms interact recursively as structurally plastic systems, ... the result is mutual ontogenic structural coupling.... For an observer, the domain of interactions specified through such ontogenic structural coupling appears as a network of sequences of mutually triggering interlocked conducts.... The various conducts or behaviors involved are both arbitrary and contextual. The behaviors are arbitrary because they can have any form as long as they operate as

---

[10]For example, see Suppes, "From behaviorism to neobehaviorism" (1975).

> triggering perturbations in the interactions; they are contextual because their participation in the interlocked interactions of the domain is defined only with respect to the interactions that constitute the domain.... I shall call the domain of interlocked conducts... a *consensual domain.*— Maturana, "Biology of language" (1978), p. 47.

For example, when the male and female of a species develop a sequence of mutual actions of approach and recognition in a mating ritual, we as observers can understand it as a coherent pattern that includes both animals. Our description is not a description of what the male and female (viewed as mechanisms made up of physical components) do, but a description of the mating dance as a pattern of mutual interactions. The generation of a consensual domain is determined by the history of states and interactions among the participants (and their progenitors) within the physical domain. However, as observers of this behavior we can distinguish a new domain in which the system of behaviors exists. The consensual domain is reducible neither to the physical domain (the structures of the organisms that participate in it) nor to the domain of interactions (the history by which it came to be), but is generated in their interplay through structural coupling as determined by the demands of autopoiesis for each participant.

Maturana refers to behavior in a consensual domain as 'linguistic behavior.' Indeed, human language is a clear example of a consensual domain, and the properties of being arbitrary and contextual have at times been taken as its defining features. But Maturana extends the term 'linguistic' to include *any* mutually generated domain of interactions. Language acts, like any other acts of an organism, can be described in the domain of structure and in the domain of cognition as well. But their existence *as language* is in the consensual domain generated by mutual interaction. A language exists among a community of individuals, and is continually regenerated through their linguistic activity and the structural coupling generated by that activity.

Language, as a consensual domain, is a patterning of 'mutual orienting behavior,' not a collection of mechanisms in a 'language user' or a 'semantic' coupling between linguistic behavior and non-linguistic perturbations experienced by the organisms.

Maturana points out that language is connotative and not denotative, and that its function is to orient the orientee within his or her cognitive domain, and not to point to independent entities. An observer will at times see a correspondence between the language observed and the entities observed, just as there is a correspondence between the frog's visual system and the existence of flies. But if we try to understand language purely within the cognitive domain, we blind ourselves to its role as orienting behavior, and make inappropriate assumptions about the necessity and nature of reference.

> The basic function of language as a system of orienting behavior is not the transmission of information or the description of an independent universe about which we can talk, but the creation of a consensual domain of behavior between linguistically interacting systems through the development of a cooperative domain of interactions.— Maturana, "Biology of language," p. 50.

The role of 'listening' in generating the meaning of an utterance is closely related to Maturana's explanation of consensual domains, and will be discussed at length in Chapter 5.

4.5 The observer and description

At this point, it is useful to take a step back and apply Maturana's orientation to what we ourselves are doing. In the act of writing down these words on paper we are engaged in linguistic activity. In using language, we are not transmitting information or describing an external universe, but are creating a cooperative domain of interactions. Our own use of language carries a possibly misleading pre-understanding.

There is a naive view (as discussed in Chapters 2 and 5) that takes language as conveying information about an objective reality. Words and sentences refer to things whose existence is independent of the act of speaking. But we ourselves are biological beings, and the thrust of Maturana's argument is that we therefore can never have knowledge about external reality. We can have a structure that reflects our history of interactions in a medium, but that medium is not composed of 'things' that are knowable. We can talk about a world, but in doing so we act as 'observers':

> An observer is a human being, a person, a living system who can make distinctions and specify that which he or she distinguishes as a unity... and is able to operate as if he or she were external to (distinct from) the circumstances in which the observer finds himself or herself. Everything said is said by an observer to another observer, who can be himself or herself.— Maturana, "Biology of language," p. 31.

As observers, we generate *distinctions* in a consensual domain. A description in any domain (whether it be the domain of goals and intention, or that of physical systems) is inevitably a statement made by an observer to another observer, and is grounded not in an external reality but in the consensual domain shared by those observers. Properties of things (in fact the recognition of distinct things at all) exist only as operational distinctions in a domain of distinctions specified by an observer. When we talk about systems and their medium, components, and structural change, we speak as if there were external things and properties. This is an inescapable result of using language, but it is always a speaking 'as if,' not an ontological claim.

This idea that all cognitive distinctions are generated by an observer (and are relative to the nature of that observer) is not new to Maturana. Köhler, for example, in his classical book *Gestalt Psychology* (1929), argued that phenomena—i.e., the way the world presents itself to the naive observer in everyday situations—are not objective or subjective by virtue of whether they arise from internal or external events, since all knowable events are in one sense internal (resulting from internal experiences and neurophysiological events). More recent work in systems theory and cybernetics[11] also challenges the naive acceptance of modes of interpretation that assume the objectivity of observation. What is different and crucial in Maturana's discourse is the recognition that distinctions lie in a consensual domain—that they presuppose some kind of social interaction in which the observer is engaged:

> The linguistic domain as a domain of orienting behavior requires at least two interacting organisms with comparable domains of interactions, so that a cooperative system of consensual interactions may be developed in which the emerging conduct of the two organisms is relevant for both.... The central feature of human existence is its occurrence in a linguistic cognitive domain. This domain is constitutively social.
> — Maturana, "Biology of cognition" (1970), pp. 41, xxiv.

In denying the possibility of subject-independent objective knowledge, Maturana does not adopt the solipsistic position that our discourse can deal ultimately only with our subjective thoughts and feelings. By virtue of being a discourse it lies in a consensual domain—a domain that exists for a social community. Reality is not objective, but neither is it individual:

> ...cultural differences do not represent different modes of treating the same objective reality, but legitimately different cognitive domains. Culturally different men live in different cognitive realities that are recursively specified through their living in them.... The question of solipsism arises only as a

---

[11]See, for example, Pask, *Conversation Theory* (1976) and *Conversation, Cognition and Learning* (1975), and von Foerster, *Cybernetics of Cybernetics* (1974).

pseudo-problem, or does not arise at all, because the necessary condition for our possibility of talking about it is our having a language that is a consensual system of interactions in a subject dependent cognitive domain, and this condition constitutes the negation of solipsism.— Maturana, "Cognitive strategies" (1974), p. 464.

In going on to deal with consciousness, Maturana again emphasizes its continuity with other phenomena of cognition, rather than seeing it as a fundamentally different capacity. He sees consciousness as generated through the operation of the consensual domain in which language is generated. Language (shared, not private) is prior to conscious thought.

4.6 Domains of explanation

The relevance of Maturana's work to the design of computers lies in his account of how biological organisms function. It was a critical perturbation to our understanding of computers because it provided a domain of concrete examples of systems that were *mechanistic* but not *programmed*. To understand the importance of this, it is useful to look at an example.

Examining a newborn baby's ability to get food, we see a remarkable collection of extremely successful behaviors. A cry gets mother's attention, the 'rooting' reflex (a light pressure on one cheek produces a head turn to that side) positions the baby's mouth over a nipple, and the sucking actions express milk. If an AI scientist set out to build such a program, he or she might propose that the baby be provided with a set of 'goals,' such as 'drink milk' and 'get nipple in mouth,' a set of 'operators' such as 'cry,' 'turn head,' and 'suck,' and a model of the world that sets them into appropriate correspondence. A more sophisticated model might even include a model of mother's goals and plans, so that the cry could be analyzed as an attempt to evoke an appropriate plan of action on her part.

But of course all of this is irrelevant to the actual mechanisms at work. The baby, like every organism, has a complex set of reflexes whose purposes can be explained in terms like those above, but whose functioning does not depend on representations, planning, or analysis. The result is behavior that is successful for a particular coupling with the medium, but is limited in its range. If the particular actions don't work, there is no generalized ability to come up with 'other ways to eat.' In Maturana's terms, we can describe behavior in either the cognitive domain (in which purposes and coupling are central) or the domain of the mechanism as a structure-determined system (in which the actual reflex paths are the key).

In trying to build computer systems, it has often been argued that we must move beyond 'baby' systems, which simply do what is appropriate because their structure is properly coupled. If the computer can manipulate an explicit model of the goals and potential actions, then it can infer possible action sequences that were not initially programmed but that lead to the desired goals. Greater flexibility should come from specifying the goals and operators instead of the course of action.

To some extent this approach is valid, but in another way it is shortsighted. It assumes that the programmer (or 'knowledge engineer') can articulate an explicit account of the system's coupling with the world— what it is intended to do, and what the consequences of its activities will be. This can be done for idealized 'toy' systems and for those with clearly circumscribed formal purposes (for example programs that calculate mathematical formulas). But the enterprise breaks down when we turn to something like a word processor, a time-sharing system, or for that matter any system with which people interact directly. No simple set of goals and operators can delimit what can and will be done. We might, for example, note that 'goals' of the word processor include allowing a person to compare two pieces of text, to rapidly skim through a document, to copy fragments from one document to another, to move quickly to some part of a document, etc. These might be satisfied by 'window' and 'scrolling' mechanisms, but they will not operate by explicit analysis of the user's goals. The person selects among basic mechanisms that the machine provides, to get the work done. If the mechanisms don't do what is needed, others may have to be added. They will often be used in ways that were not anticipated in their design.

Similarly, the effects of different 'operators' cannot be fully described or anticipated when they elicit responses by people (or even by other computer systems). We can define the domain of perturbations (the space of possible effects the interaction can have on the system), but we cannot model how the system's activity will engender them.

The most successful designs are not those that try to fully model the domain in which they operate, but those that are 'in alignment' with the fundamental structure of that domain, and that allow for modification and evolution to generate new structural coupling. As observers (and programmers), we want to understand to the best of our ability just what the relevant domain of action is. This understanding guides our design and selection of structural changes, but need not (and in fact cannot) be embodied in the form of the mechanism.

In Chapters 8 and 12 we will explore more fully the consequences of Maturana's approach for the design of computer programs, and for the discourse about machines and intelligence.

Chapter 5

Language, listening, and commitment

The third foundation on which we will build our understanding of computers is a theory of language that combines the hermeneutic orientation of Chapter 3 with the theory of *speech acts*—the analysis of language as meaningful acts by speakers in situations of shared activity. In this chapter we show how 'language as action' and 'language as interpretation' can be reconciled. In doing this we will move back and forth between two fundamental questions: "How does an utterance have meaning?" and "What kinds of actions do we perform in language?" The juxtaposition of these questions leads us to a new grounding for our understanding of language and the nature of human existence as language.

5.1 Listening in a background

Chapter 2 introduced the concept of 'literal meaning' and its importance to rationalistic semantic theories. Searle characterizes what he sees as the 'received opinion:'

> Sentences have literal meanings. The literal meaning of a sentence is entirely determined by the meanings of its component words (or morphemes) and the syntactical rules according to which these elements are combined.... For sentences in the indicative, the meaning of a sentence determines a set of truth conditions; that is, it determines a set of conditions such that the literal utterance of the sentence to make a statement will be the making of a true statement if and only if those conditions

are satisfied.... The literal meaning of the sentence is the meaning it has independently of any context whatever; and, diachronic changes [changes in the language over time] apart, it keeps that meaning in any context in which it is uttered. — Searle, "Literal meaning" (1979), p. 117.

Formal analytic approaches based on literal meaning often take as their model the language of mathematics, in which the truth of a statement can be determined without reference to outside context or situation.[1] But in real language, one rarely if ever makes a statement that could not be construed as having an unintended literal meaning. Speaker A says "Snow is white" and B can point to the murky grey polluted stuff at their feet. A replies "I meant pure snow," and B responds "You didn't say so, and anyway no snow is absolutely pure." It is an edifying exercise to look at the statements made both in writing and in everyday conversation, to see how few of them can even apparently be judged true or false without an appeal to an unstated background.

It is impossible to establish a context-independent basis for circumscribing the literal use of a term even as seemingly simple as "water," as shown by the following dialog:

A: Is there any water in the refrigerator?
B: Yes.
A: Where? I don't see it.
B: In the cells of the eggplant.

A claims that B's first response was a lie (or at best 'misleading'), while B contends that it was literally true. Most semantic theories in the rationalistic tradition provide formal grounds to support B, but a theory of language as a human phenomenon needs to deal with the grounds for A's complaint as well—i.e., with the 'infelicity' of B's reply.

At first, it seems that it might be possible simply to expand the definition of "water." Perhaps there is a 'sense' of the word that means "water in its liquid phase in sufficient quantity to act as a fluid," so that a sentence containing the word "water" is ambiguous as to whether it refers to this sense or to a sense dealing purely with chemical composition. But this doesn't help us in dealing with some other possible responses of B:

1. B: Yes, condensed on the bottom of the cooling coils.

2. B: There's no water in the refrigerator, but there's some lemonade.

---

[1]In fact, as pointed out by Lakatos in *Proofs and Refutations* (1976), this is not really the case even in mathematics.

3. B: Yes, there's a bottle of water in the refrigerator, with a little lemon in it to cover up the taste of the rust from the pipes.

Response 1 is facetious, like the one about eggplants. But that is only because of background. It might be appropriate if person A were checking for sources of humidity that ruined some photographic plates being stored in the refrigerator. Similarly, in responses 2 and 3, subtle cultural issues are at stake in deciding whether a certain amount of lemon should disqualify a substance as being "water." We cannot come up with a situation-independent definition of what qualifies as water, since after any amount of fiddling with the definition, one can always come up with a new context in which it is inadequate. In making the statement "There's some water in the refrigerator," a person is not stating an objective fact. Every speech act occurs in a context, with a background shared by speaker and hearer. The 'felicity conditions' depend on mutual knowledge and intentions.

Some other simple examples illustrate a variety of ways in which the background can be relevant.

1. Joan has never failed a student in Linguistics 265.

2. I'm sorry I missed the meeting yesterday. My car had a flat tire.

3. There's an animal over there in the bushes.

Sentence 1 is formally true in many circumstances, including the one in which Joan has never taught Linguistics 265. However, in ordinary conversation, the hearer makes the additional inference that Joan has taught the course, and is justified in accusing the speaker of bad faith if the inference is not true. Similarly in sentence 2, the hearer assumes that there is a coherence to the events being described. If the second sentence were "There are fifteen million people in Mexico City," the hearer would be puzzled, and if the flat tire had nothing to do with missing the meeting (even though it actually was flat), the speaker is practicing deception. Sentence 3 is a more subtle case. If the hearer looks over and sees a dog in the bushes, and finds out that the speaker knew it was a dog, he or she will feel that the statement was inappropriate, and might say "If you knew it was a dog, why didn't you say so?" On the other hand, the statement "There's a dog over there in the bushes" is perfectly appropriate even if both speaker and hearer know that it is a beagle, and sentence 3 would be fine for a dog if it were a response to something like "There are no animals anywhere around here."

Austin (whose work on speech acts is described below) summed matters up as follows:

> It is essential to realize that 'true' and 'false,' like 'free' and
> 'unfree,' do not stand for anything simple at all; but only for
> a general dimension of being a right or proper thing to say
> as opposed to a wrong thing, in these circumstances, to this
> audience, for these purposes, and with these intentions. —
> Austin, *How to Do Things with Words* (1962), p. 145.

There have been attempts to give theoretical accounts of these phenomena. Some, such as Grice's conversational principles ("Logic and conversation," 1975), are in the form of 'pragmatic' rules followed by speakers
of a language. Others, such as Rosch's analysis of human categorization
systems,[2] look toward psychological explanations. Moravcsik ("How do
words get their meanings," 1981) has proposed 'aitiational schemes,' which
include functional and causal factors in defining meaning. Although such
analyses point to important phenomena, they cannot provide a full account of background and the listening that lives within it. To do so they
would have to make explicit the conditions that distinguish those situations in which the use of a particular word or phrase is appropriate. For
example, in Searle's paper on literal meaning, truth conditions still play a
central role, although they are seen as relative to a background:

> For a large class of unambiguous sentences such as "The cat is
> on the mat," the notion of the literal meaning of the sentence
> only has application relative to a set of background assump-
> tions. The truth conditions of the sentence will vary with vari-
> ations in these background assumptions; and given the absence
> or presence of some background assumptions the sentence does
> not have determinate truth conditions. These variations have
> nothing to do with indexicality, change of meaning, ambigu-
> ity, conversational implication, vagueness or presupposition as
> these notions are standardly discussed in the philosophical and
> linguistic literature. — Searle, "Literal meaning" (1979), p. 125.

We must be cautious with this statement. In speaking of 'a set of background assumptions,' Searle suggests that background can be accounted
for by adding the appropriate set of further propositions to a formal semantic account. As we argued in Chapter 3, however, background is a
pervasive and fundamental phenomenon. Background is the space of possibilities that allows us to listen to both what is spoken and what is unspoken. Meaning is created by an active listening, in which the linguistic
form triggers interpretation, rather than conveying information. The background is not a set of propositions, but is our basic orientation of 'care'

---

[2] The example of Sentence 3 above is like those studied in Rosch, "Cognitive representations of semantic categories" (1975).

for the world. This world is always already organized around fundamental human projects, and depends upon these projects for its being and organization.

To recapitulate in more explicitly Heideggerian language, the world is encountered as something always already lived in, worked in, and acted upon. World as the background of obviousness is manifest in our everyday dealings as the familiarity that pervades our situation, and every possible utterance presupposes this. Listening for our possibilities in a world in which we already dwell allows us to speak and to elicit the cooperation of others. That which is not obvious is made manifest through language. What is unspoken is as much a part of the meaning as what is spoken.

5.2   Meaning, commitment, and speech acts

Having posed the problem of meaning, we turn for a moment to the structure of language acts. In doing so, we draw on speech act theory, as originated by the philosopher J. L. Austin (*How to Do Things with Words*, 1962). Austin studied a class of utterances (which he termed 'performatives') that do not refer to states of the world, but that in themselves constitute acts such as promising, threatening, and naming. He argued that the generally accepted view of the truth and falsity of propositions was not applicable to many of these speech acts. It does not make sense to ask whether a particular utterance of "I pronounce you man and wife" or "Get me a hamburger" is true or false, but rather whether it is *felicitous*— whether it is appropriate to the context in which it is uttered.

Austin's student Searle (*Speech Acts*, 1969) formalized the structure of the felicity conditions associated with a variety of speech acts, such as promising and requesting. In "A taxonomy of illocutionary acts" (1975) he classified all speech acts as embodying one of five fundamental *illocutionary points*. These categories cover all utterances, not just sentences with explicit performative verbs such as "I promise..." and "I declare..." For example, we can talk about a speech act as being a promise even though its form may be a simple statement, as in "I'll be there."

The five categories of illocutionary point are:

Assertives: commit the speaker (in varying degrees) to something's being the case—to the truth of the expressed proposition.

Directives: attempt (in varying degrees) to get the hearer to do something. These include both questions (which can direct the hearer to make an assertive speech act in response) and commands (which attempt to get the hearer to carry out some linguistic or non-linguistic act).

Commissives: commit the speaker (again in varying degrees) to some future course of action.

Expressives: express a psychological state about a state of affairs. This class includes acts such as apologizing and praising.

Declarations: bring about the correspondence between the propositional content of the speech act and reality, as illustrated by the example of pronouncing a couple married.

Searle distinguishes among the *illocutionary point* of an utterance, its *illocutionary force*, and its *propositional content*. The illocutionary point is one of the five categories above. Two speech acts (such as a polite question and a demand for information) may differ in their illocutionary force (manner and degree) while having the same illocutionary point (in this case a directive). The fact that an utterance involves a proposition about some topic, such as the speaker's attendance at a particular meeting at a particular time, is its propositional content.

The essential importance of illocutionary point is the specification of meaning in terms of patterns of commitment entered into by speaker and hearer by virtue of taking part in the conversation. The taxonomy classifies the possibilities for what a speaker can *do* with an utterance. It is not a set of cultural conventions like those governing polite behavior. It is based on the underlying set of possibilities for how words can be related to the world. Each culture or language may have its unique ways of expressing the different speech acts, but the space of possibilities is the universal basis of our existence in language.

The centrality of commitment in speech act theory has been brought out particularly clearly by Habermas in discussing what he calls the 'validity claims' of an utterance:

> The essential presupposition for the success of an illocutionary act consists in the speaker's entering into a specific *engagement*, so that the hearer can rely on him. An utterance can count as a promise, assertion, request, question, or avowal, if and only if the speaker makes an offer that he is ready to make good insofar as it is accepted by the hearer. The speaker must engage himself, that is, indicate that in certain situations he will draw certain consequences for action. — Habermas, "What is universal pragmatics?" (1979), p. 61.

Habermas argues that every language act has consequences for the participants, leading to other immediate actions and to commitments for future action. In making a statement, a speaker is doing something like making a promise—making a commitment to act in appropriate ways in the future. Of course, a statement has a different kind of satisfaction condition from a promise. No specific action is anticipated, but there is a structure of potential dialog in the face of a breakdown. If the speaker says "Yes, there is water in the refrigerator" and the hearer can't find any, the speaker is committed to give an account. Either they reach agreement that the statement was inappropriate, or they articulate part of the assumed background ("I thought you were looking for something to drink," "I assumed we were talking about chemical composition.")

Speech act theory, then, recognizes the importance of commitment and is a first step towards dealing more adequately with meaning. But as we have described it so far, it does not go outside of the rationalistic tradition. Our emphasis on interpretation and background was not part of that theory as originally developed and is not shared by all those currently working on it. Much of the work on speech acts attempts to extend rather than reject the notion that the meaning of an utterance can be described in terms of conditions stated independently of context. For example, in precisely specifying the 'sincerity conditions' that are necessary for an act of promising, one must refer to the intentional states of the speaker (e.g., the speaker believes that it is possible to do the promised act and intends to do it). In extending simple truth-conditional accounts to include mental states, one is still treating the conditions of appropriate meaning as though it were an objective state of affairs. In order to understand how meaning is shared, we must look at the social rather than the mental dimension.

5.3 Objectivity and tradition

Readers with a background in the rationalistic tradition may well be getting impatient at this point. Surely there must be some way of talking about meaning that isn't tied up with the fuzziness of background and social commitment. If the meaning of an utterance can be described only in terms of its interpretation by a particular speaker or listener in a particular situation with a particular history, how do we talk about regularities of meaning at all? Since no two situations are identical and no two people have identical histories, we are in danger of being left with no grounds for generalization. If every aspect of the situation or of the individual backgrounds can potentially bear on a meaning, how can we talk about regularities that go across situations and speakers?

As a simple example, consider the appropriateness of using a common noun, such as "dog," in referring to a particular object of interest or using the preposition "on" to describe a relationship between two objects. The naive view of language is that it simply reflects reality. Nature (or at least nature as perceived by the human organism) comes carved up into objects of various kinds, and the role of language is to give them labels and to state facts about them. A language can be arbitrary in using the words "dog" and "on" or *"chien"* and *"sur,"* but it is constrained by the nature of the world to group a certain set of objects or properties together under whichever names it uses.

As long as we stick to the rather idealized isolated sentences used as examples in philosophy books, it may seem plausible to ground the meaning of words in a language-prior categorization. Whether a given object is a "bachelor" or a "lemon" is taken to be a matter of definition or of science, not one of utterance context. But as soon as we look at real situated language, the foundation crumbles. Examples like the ones in the previous sections usually convince people that the naive view of language as description cannot account for the way they actually use language (although some will continue to maintain that it accounts for the way people *should* use language).

But even many sophisticated linguists and philosophers are genuinely puzzled when one proposes that the basis for the meaning of words and sentences is not ultimately definable in terms of an objective external world. There may be some difficult cases, but most of the time for most purposes, the correspondence seems pretty close to what you would naively expect. How can we reconcile this with our emphasis on interpretation and the generation of meaning through listening within a situation?

Consider an analogy: the study of roads and their relation to the terrain. Looking at a roadmap superimposed on a topographic map, one sees tremendous regularities. Roads follow along riverbeds, they go through passes, and they wind their way up and down mountainsides in a regular fashion. Surely this regularity must mean that road placement is determined by the lay of the land. But of course it isn't. The road network is conditioned by the lay of the land, and it would be strange (though certainly not impossible, given modern technology) to cut from here to there in total disregard of the terrain. But the actual placement depends on who wants to get vehicles of what kind from where to where, for reasons that transcend geography.

Words correspond to our intuition about 'reality' because our purposes in using them are closely aligned with our physical existence in a world and our actions within it. But the coincidence is the result of our use of language within a tradition (or, as Maturana might say, our structural coupling within a consensual domain).

Language and cognition are fundamentally social. Maturana, Gadamer, and Heidegger all argue that our ability to think and to give meaning to language is rooted in our participation in a society and a tradition. Heidegger emphasizes that the meaning and organization of a culture must be taken as the basic given and cannot be traced back to the meaning-giving activity of individual subjects. Habermas is explicit in relating meaning to an extended kind of cultural agreement.

> I may ascribe a predicate to an object if and only if every other person who could enter into a dialogue with me would ascribe the same predicate to the same object. In order to distinguish true from false statements, I make reference to the judgment of others—in fact to the judgment of all others with whom I could ever hold a dialogue (among whom I counterfactually include all the dialogue partners I could find if my life history were coextensive with the history of mankind). The condition of the truth of statements is the potential agreements of all others. — Habermas, "Wahrheitstheorien" [Theories of truth] (1973), p. 220.

Habermas's imagined infinite dialog is a valuable metaphor, but does not provide us with useful structure. We can never have this infinity of hypothetical dialogs, and even among those we could have, we would not find absolute agreement. It would be ontologically vacuous to modify Habermas's idealization in some kind of statistical or probabilistic direction, attributing meaning to a sort of 'popularity poll.'[3] Maturana's theory of structural coupling furnishes a more revealing analogy.

Through structural coupling, an organism comes to have a structure that allows it to function successfully within its medium. The demands of continued autopoiesis shape this structure in a way that can be viewed as a reflection of an external world. But the correspondence is not one in which the form of the world is somehow mapped onto the structure of the organism. It is indirect (and partial), as created by the results of actions produced by the structure, and their potential to lead to breakdown—to the disintegration of the organism.

In language, the correspondence of words to our non-linguistic medium is equally indirect. We use language in human activities, and our use of linguistic forms is shaped by the need for effective coordination of action with others. If one person's utterance is not intelligible to others, or if its interpretation by the listener is not consistent with the actions the speaker anticipates, there will be a breakdown. This breakdown may not be as drastic as those in the biological domain (although at times it will be), but in any case it results in the loss of mutual trust in commitment. If I say there is water in the refrigerator and this assertion is not consistent

---

[3]It is also not adequate to do as Putnam suggests in "Is semantics possible?" (1970), locating 'real' meaning in the usage of the 'experts' who deal with scientific terms. Our "water" examples demonstrate that this deals with meaning only in a specialized and limited sense.

with the domain of relevant actions, you may decide that you can't "take me seriously" or "believe what I say." A fundamental condition of successful communication is lost. The need for continued mutual recognition of commitment plays the role analogous to the demands of autopoiesis in selecting among possible sequences of behaviors.

From this analogy we can see how language can work without any 'objective' criteria of meaning. We need not base our use of a particular word on any externally determined truth conditions, and need not even be in full agreement with our language partners on the situations in which it would be appropriate. All that is required is that there be a sufficient coupling so that breakdowns are infrequent, and a standing commitment by both speaker and listener to enter into dialog in the face of a breakdown.[4]

The conditions of appropriateness for commitment naturally take into account the role of a shared unarticulated background. When a person promises to do something, it goes without saying that the commitment is relative to unstated assumptions. If someone asks me to come to a meeting tomorrow and I respond "I'll be there," I am performing a commissive speech act. By virtue of the utterance, I create a commitment. If I find out tomorrow that the meeting has been moved to Timbuktu and don't show up, I can justifiably argue that I haven't broken my promise. What I really meant was "Assuming it is held as scheduled. . ." On the other hand, if the meeting is moved to an adjacent room, and I know it but don't show up, you are justified in arguing that I have broken my promise, and that the 'Timbuktu excuse' doesn't apply. The same properties carry over to all language acts: meaning is relative to what is understood through the tradition.

It may appear that there is a conflict between our emphasis on meaning as commitment and on the active interpretive role of the listener. If the meaning of a speech act is created by listening within a background, how can the speaker be responsible for a commitment to its consequences? But of course, there is no contradiction, just as there is no contradiction in the preceding example of a promise. As participants in a shared tradition, we are each responsible for the consequences of how our acts will be understood within that tradition. The fact that there are no objective rules and that there may at times be disagreements does not free us of that responsibility.

---

[4] A similar insight was put forth in discussions of meaning ('semiotics') by the pragmatists, such as Peirce, Dewey and Mead. As John-Steiner and Tatter ("An interactionist model of language development," 1983) describe the pragmatist orientation: "The semiotic process is purposive, having a directed flow. It functions to choreograph and to harmonize the mutual adjustments necessary for the carrying out of human social activities. It has its sign function only within the intentional context of social cooperation and direction, in which past and future phases of activity are brought to bear upon the present."

5.4   Recurrence and formalization

In a complete rationalistic analysis of meaning, we would be able to explicate the meaning of each utterance by showing how it is built up systematically from smaller elements, each with its own determinate meaning. At the bottom, the smallest elements would denote objects, properties, and relations of interest in the external world. Although there is a deep fallacy in this orientation, there is also a power in its emphasis on regular formal structures. To the extent that they are adequate for a particular purpose (such as the implementation of language-like facilities on computers) they provide a systematic approach for generating rules and operations dealing with symbolic representations.

Having observed that the regularities in the use of language grow out of mutual coupling among language users (not the coupling of the individual to some external reality), we are faced with the question of how to apply rigorous methods in our accounts of meaning. We will not expect to find networks of definitions, either stipulated or empirically determined, by which we can determine the truth conditions associated with utterances and their constituent parts. But this does not mean there are no regularities, or that formal accounts are useless. In our introduction we observed that computers can play a major role as devices for facilitating human communication in language. As we will see in Part II, computer programming is based on the ability to observe and describe regular recurrences.

The issue here is one of finding the appropriate *domain of recurrence.* Linguistic behavior can be described in several distinct domains. The relevant regularities are not in individual speech acts (embodied in sentences) or in some kind of explicit agreement about meanings. They appear in the domain of conversation, in which successive speech acts are related to one another. This domain is like Maturana's cognitive domain, in being relational and historical. The regularities do not appear in the correlation between an act and the structure of the actor, but in the relevance of a pattern of acts through time.

As an example of conversational analysis we will consider in some detail the network of speech acts that constitute straightforward *conversations for action*—those in which an interplay of requests and commissives are directed towards explicit cooperative action. This is a useful example both because of its clarity and because it is the basis for computer tools for conducting conversations, as described in Chapter 11.

We can plot the basic course of a conversation in a simple diagram like that of Figure 5.1, in which each circle represents a possible state of the conversation and the lines represent speech acts. This is not a model of the mental state of a speaker or hearer, but shows the conversation as a 'dance.'

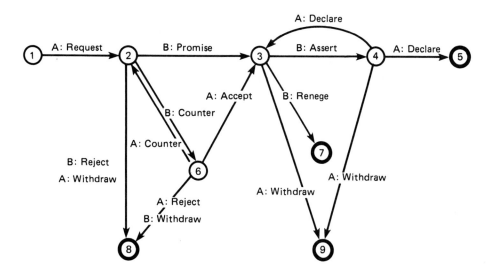

Figure 5.1: The basic conversation for action

The lines indicate actions that can be taken by the initial speaker (A) and hearer (B). The initial action is a request from A to B, which specifies some *conditions of satisfaction*. Following such a request, there are precisely five alternatives: the hearer can accept the conditions (promising to satisfy them), can reject them, or can ask to negotiate a change in the conditions of satisfaction (counteroffer). The original speaker can also withdraw the request before a response, or can modify its conditions.[5]

Each action in turn leads to a different state, with its own space of possibilities. In the 'normal' course of events, B at some point asserts to A that the conditions of satisfaction have been met (moving to the state labelled 4 in the figure). If A declares that he or she is satisfied, the conversation reaches a successful completion (state 5). On the other hand, A may not interpret the situation in the same way and may declare that the conditions have not been met, returning the conversation to state 3. In this state, either party may propose a change to the conditions of satisfaction, and in any state one or the other party may back out on the deal, moving to a state of completion in which one or the other can be

---

[5]These are the acts directly relevant to the structure of completion of the conversation for action. There are of course other possibilities in which the conversational acts themselves are taken as a topic, for example in questioning the intelligibility ("What, I didn't hear you") or legitimacy ("You can't order me to do that!") of the acts.

held 'liable' (states 7 and 9).

Several points about this conversation structure deserve note:

1. At each point in the conversation, there is a small set of possible actions determined by the previous history. We are concerned here with the basic structure, not the details of content. For example, the action 'counteroffer' includes any number of possibilities for just what the new conditions of satisfaction are to be.

2. All of the relevant acts are linguistic—they represent utterances by the parties to the conversation or silences that are listened to as standing for an act. The act that follows a commitment is an assertion (an assertive speech act) from the original hearer to the requestor that the request has been satisfied, and must be followed by a declaration by the requestor that it is satisfactory. The actual doing of whatever is needed to meet the conditions of satisfaction lies outside of the conversation.

3. There are many cases where acts are 'listened to' without being explicit. If the requestor can recognize satisfaction of the request directly, there may be no explicit assertion of completion. Other acts, such as declaring satisfaction, may be taken for granted if some amount of time goes by without a declaration to the contrary. What is not said is listened to as much as what is said.

4. Conditions of satisfaction are not objective realities, free of the interpretations of speaker and hearer. They exist in the listening, and there is always the potential for a difference among the parties. This can lead to breakdown (for example, when the promiser declares that the commitment is satisfied, and the requestor does not agree) and to a subsequent conversation about the understanding of the conditions.

5. There are a few states of 'completion' from which no further actions can be taken (these are the heavy circles in the figure). All other states represent an incomplete conversation. Completion does not guarantee satisfaction. For example, if the promiser takes the action of 'reneging,' the conversation moves to a completed state, in which the original request was not satisfied.

6. The network does not say what people *should* do, or deal with consequences of the acts (such as backing out of a commitment). These are important phenomena in human situations, but are not generated in the domain of conversation formalized in this network.

The analysis illustrated by this network can then be used as a basis for further dimensions of recurrent structure in conversations. These include temporal relations among the speech acts, and the linking of conversations with each other (for example, a request is issued in order to help in the satisfaction of some promise previously made by the requestor). These will be discussed further in Chapter 11.

Other kinds of conversations can be analyzed in a similar vein. For example, in order to account for the truthfulness of assertives in the domain of recurrent structures of conversation, we need a 'logic of argument,' where 'argument' stands for the sequence of speech acts relevant to the articulation of background assumptions. When one utters a statement, one is committed to provide some kind of 'grounding' in case of a breakdown. This grounding is in the form of another speech act (also in a situational context) to satisfy the hearer that the objection is met. There are three basic kinds of grounding: experiential, formal, and social.

Experiential. If asked to justify the statement "Snow is white," one can give a set of instructions ("Go outside and look!") such that any person who follows them will be led to concur on the basis of experience. The methodology of science is designed to provide this kind of grounding for all empirical statements. Maturana points out that the so-called 'objectivity' of science derives from the assumption that for any observation, one can provide instructions that if followed by a 'standard observer' will lead him or her to the same conclusion. This does not necessarily mean that the result is observer-free, simply that it is anticipated to be uniform for all potential human observers.

Formal. Deductive logic and mathematics are based on the playing of a kind of 'language game'[6] in which a set of formal rules is taken for granted and argument proceeds as a series of moves constrained by those rules. For example, if I expect you to believe that all Swedes are blonde and that Sven is a redhead, then I can use a particular series of moves to provide grounding for the statement that Sven is not Swedish. Of course, one can recursively demand grounding for each of the statements used in the process until some non-formal grounding is reached. Formal grounding is the subject matter of formal compositional semantics, but with a different emphasis. Our focus here is not on the coherence of a mathematical abstraction but on how the formal structures play a role in patterns of conversation.

---

[6] In a series of papers such as "Quantifiers in logic and quantifiers in natural languages" (1976), Hintikka uses games as a basis for a form of deductive logic, including modal logic. Wittgenstein's *Philosophical Investigations* (1963) introduced the term 'language game' in a somewhat different but related sense.

Social. Much of what we say in conversation is based neither on experience nor on logic, but on other conversations. We believe that water is H_2O and that Napoleon was the Emperor of France not because we have relevant experience but because someone told us. One possible form of grounding is to 'pass the buck'—to argue that whoever made the statement could have provided grounding.

Just as one can develop taxonomies and structural analyses of illocutionary points, it is important to develop a precise analysis of these structures of argumentation. There are many ways in which such a logic will parallel standard formal logic, and others in which it will not. For example, the role of analogy and metaphor will be more central when the focus is on patterns of discourse between individuals with a shared background rather than on deductive inference from axioms.[7]

In our examination of these recurrent patterns of conversation we must keep in mind that they exist in the domain of the observed conversation, not in some mental domain of the participants. A speaker and hearer do not apply 'conversation pattern rules' any more than they apply 'perception rules' or 'deduction rules.' As emphasized in Chapter 3, the essential feature of language activity (the processes of saying and listening) is the thrownness of a person within language. When we are engaged in successful language activity, the conversation is not present-at-hand, as something observed. We are immersed in its unfolding. Its structure becomes visible only when there is some kind of breakdown.

5.5   Breakdown, language, and existence

So far in this chapter we have emphasized two main points:

1. Meaning arises in listening to the commitment expressed in speech acts.

2. The articulation of content—how we talk about the world—emerges in recurrent patterns of breakdown and the potential for discourse about grounding.

From these points, we are led to a more radical recognition about language and existence: *Nothing exists except through language.*

We must be careful in our understanding. We are not advocating a linguistic solipsism that denies our embedding in a world outside of our speaking. What is crucial is the nature of 'existing.' In saying that some

---

[7]For a discussion of the central role that metaphor plays in language use, see Lakoff and Johnson, *Metaphors We Live By* (1980).

'thing' exists (or that it has some property), we have brought it into a domain of articulated objects and qualities that exists in language and through the structure of language, constrained by our potential for action in the world.

As an example, let us look once again at the meaning of individual words, and the problem of how a particular choice of words is appropriate in a situation. We have shown how "water" can have different interpretations in different situations, but how does it come to have the same interpretation in more than one? The distinctions made by language are not determined by some objective classification of 'situations' in the world, but neither are they totally arbitrary.[8] Distinctions arise from recurrent patterns of breakdown in concernful activity. There are a variety of human activities, including drinking, putting out fires, and washing, for which the absence or presence of "water" determines a space of potential breakdowns. Words arise to help anticipate and cope with these breakdowns. It is often remarked that the Eskimos have a large number of distinctions for forms of snow. This is not just because they see a lot of snow (we see many things we don't bother talking about), but precisely because there are recurrent activities with spaces of potential breakdown for which the distinctions are relevant.

It is easy to obscure this insight by considering only examples that fall close to simple recurrences of physical activity and sensory experience. It naively seems that somehow "snow" must exist as a specific kind of entity regardless of any language (or even human experience) about it. On the other hand, it is easy to find examples that cannot be conceived of as existing outside the domain of human commitment and interaction, such as "friendship," "crisis," and "semantics." In this chapter we have chosen to focus on words like "water" instead of more explicitly socially-grounded words, precisely because the apparent simplicity of physically-interpreted terms is misleading.

We will see in Part II that this apparently paradoxical view (that nothing exists except through language) gives us a practical orientation for understanding and designing computer systems. The domain in which people need to understand the operation of computers goes beyond the physical composition of their parts, into areas of structure and behavior for which naive views of objects and properties are clearly inadequate. The 'things' that make up 'software,' 'interfaces,' and 'user interactions' are clear examples of entities whose existence and properties are generated in the language and commitment of those who build and discuss them.

---

[8] Winograd, in "Moving the semantic fulcrum" (1985), criticizes the assumptions made by Barwise and Perry in basing their theory of 'situation semantics' (*Situations and Attitudes*, 1983) on a naive realism that takes for granted the existence of specific objects and properties independent of language.

Chapter 6

Towards a new orientation

The previous chapters have dealt with fundamental questions of what it means to exist as a human being, capable of thought and language. Our discourse concerning these questions grew out of seeing their direct relevance to our understanding of computers and the possibilities for the design of new computer technology. We do not have the pretension of creating a grand philosophical synthesis in which Maturana, Heidegger, Gadamer, Austin, Searle, and others all find a niche. The importance of their work lies in its potential for unconcealing the rationalistic tradition in which we are already immersed. Their unity lies in the elements of the tradition that they challenge, and thereby reveal.

As background to our study of computers and programming in Part II, this section summarizes the concerns raised in previous chapters, pointing out their areas of overlap and the role they play in our detailed examination of computer technology and design.

6.1 Cognition and being in the world

This book has the word 'cognition' in its title, and in the previous chapters we have given accounts of cognitive activity. But in using the term 'cognition' we fall into the danger of implicitly following the tradition that we are challenging. In labelling it as a distinct function like 'respiration' or 'locomotion,' we evoke an understanding that an activity of 'cognizing' can be separated from the rest of the activity of the organism. We need first to examine this understanding more carefully and to recognize its consequences for design.

In speaking of thinking as a kind of activity, we adopt a common pre-understanding that seems so obvious as to be unarguable. When you sit at your desk deciding where to go for lunch, it seems clear that you are engaged in 'thinking,' as opposed to other things you might be doing at the time. This activity can be characterized in terms of mental states and mental operations. An explanation of how it is carried out will be couched in terms of sentences and representations, concepts, and ideas. This kind of detached reflection is obviously a part of what people do. The blindness of the rationalistic tradition lies in assuming that it can serve as a basis for understanding the full range of what we might call 'cognition.' Each of the previous three chapters challenges this assumption.

One of the most fundamental aspects of Heidegger's discourse is his emphasis on the state of thrownness as a condition of being-in-the-world. We do at times engage in conscious reflection and systematic thought, but these are secondary to the pre-reflective experience of being thrown in a situation in which we are always already acting. We are always engaged in acting within a situation, without the opportunity to fully disengage ourselves and function as detached observers. Even what we call 'disengagement' occurs within thrownness: we do not escape our thrownness, but shift our domain of concern. Our acts always happen within thrownness and cannot be understood as the results of a process (conscious or non-conscious) of representing, planning, and reasoning.

Heidegger argues that our being-in-the-world is not a detached reflection on the external world as present-at-hand, but exists in the readiness-to-hand of the world as it is unconcealed in our actions. Maturana, through his examination of biological systems, arrived in a different way at a remarkably similar understanding. He states that our ability to function as observers is generated from our functioning as structure-determined systems, shaped by structural coupling. Every organism is engaged in a pattern of activity that is triggered by changes in its medium, and that has the potential to change the structure of the organism (and hence to change its future behavior).

Both authors recognize and analyze the phenomena that have generated our naive view of the connection between thinking and acting, and both argue that we must go beyond this view if we want to understand the nature of cognition—cognition viewed not as activity in some mental realm, but as a pattern of behavior that is relevant to the functioning of the person or organism in its world.

When we look at computer technology, this basic point guides our understanding in several ways. First, it is critical in our anticipation of the kinds of computer tools that will be useful. In a tradition that emphasizes thought as an independent activity, we will tend to design systems to work within that domain. In fact much of the current advertising rhetoric about computers stresses the role they will play in 'applying knowledge' and 'making decisions.' If, on the other hand, we take action as primary, we will ask how computers can play a role in the kinds of actions that make up our lives—particularly the communicative acts that create requests and commitments and that serve to link us to others. The discussion of word processors in Chapter 1 (which pointed out the computer's role in a network of equipment and social interactions) illustrates how we can gain a new perspective on already existing systems and shape the direction of future ones.

We also want to better understand how people use computers. The rationalistic tradition emphasizes the role played by analytical understanding and reasoning in the process of interacting with our world, including our tools. Heidegger and Maturana, in their own ways, point to the importance of readiness-to-hand (structural coupling) and the ways in which objects and properties come into existence when there is an unreadiness or breakdown in that coupling. From this standpoint, the designer of a computer tool must work in the domain generated by the space of potential breakdowns. The current emphasis on creating 'user-friendly' computers is an expression of the implicit recognition that earlier systems were not designed with this domain sufficiently in mind. A good deal of wisdom has been gained through experience in the practical design of systems, and one of our goals is to provide a clearer theoretical foundation on which to base system design. We will come back to this issue in our discussion of design in Chapter 12.

Finally, our orientation to cognition and action has a substantial impact on the way we understand computer programs that are characterized by their designers as 'thinking' and 'making decisions.' The fact that such labels can be applied seriously at all is a reflection of the rationalistic tradition. In Chapters 8 through 10, we will examine work in artificial intelligence, arguing that the current popular discourse on questions like "Can computers think?" needs to be reoriented.

6.2   Knowledge and representation

Our understanding of being is closely linked to our understanding of knowledge. The question of what it means to know is one of the oldest and most central issues of philosophy, and one that is at the heart of Heidegger's challenge. Chapter 2 described a 'naive realism' that is prominent within the rationalistic tradition. As we pointed out there, this is not a logical consequence of the tradition (and is not accepted by all philosophers within it), but it is part of the pervasive background that follows the tradition in our everyday understanding.

At its simplest, the rationalistic view accepts the existence of an objective reality, made up of things bearing properties and entering into relations. A cognitive being 'gathers information' about those things and builds up a 'mental model' which will be in some respects correct (a faithful representation of reality) and in other respects incorrect. Knowledge is a storehouse of representations, which can be called upon for use in reasoning and which can be translated into language. Thinking is a process of manipulating representations.

This naive ontology and epistemology is one of the central issues for both Maturana and Heidegger. Neither of them accepts the existence of 'things' that are the bearers of properties independently of interpretation. They argue that we can not talk coherently of an 'external' world, but are always concerned with interpretation. Maturana describes the nervous system as closed, and argues against the appropriateness of terms like 'perception' and 'information.' Heidegger begins with being-in-the-world, observing that present-at-hand objects emerge from a more fundamental state of being in which readiness-to-hand does not distinguish objects or properties.

For Heidegger, 'things' emerge in breakdown, when unreadiness-to-hand unconceals them as a matter of concern. Maturana sees the presence of objects and properties as relevant only in a domain of distinctions made by an observer. In the domain of biological mechanism they do not exist. Both authors recognize that we are situated in a world that is not of our own making. Their central insight is that this world, constituted as a world of objects and properties, arises only in the concernful activities of the person.

Maturana and Heidegger both oppose the assumption that cognition is based on the manipulation of mental models or representations of the world, although they do so on very different grounds. Maturana begins as a biologist, examining the workings of the nervous system. He argues that while there is a domain of description (the cognitive domain) in which it is appropriate to talk about the correspondence between effective behavior and the structure of the medium in which it takes place, we must not confuse this domain of description with the domain of structural (biological) mechanisms that operate to produce behavior. In saying that a representation is present in the nervous system, we are indulging in misplaced concreteness, and can easily be led into fruitless quests for the corresponding mechanisms. While the point is obvious in cases of reflex behavior like the frog and fly of his early research, Maturana sees it as central to our understanding of all behavior, including complex cognitive and linguistic activities.

Heidegger makes a more radical critique, questioning the distinction between a conscious, reflective, knowing 'subject' and a separable 'object.'

He sees representation as a derivative phenomenon, which occurs only when there is a breaking down of our concernful action. Knowledge lies in the being that situates us in the world, not in a reflective representation.

Chapter 2 described efforts being made to create a unified 'cognitive science,' concerned with cognition in people, animals, and machines. To the extent that there is intellectual unity in this quest, it centers around some form of the *representation hypothesis:* the assumption that cognition rests on the manipulation of symbolic representations that can be understood as referring to objects and properties in the world.[1]

When we turn to a careful examination of computer systems in Chapter 7, we will see that the corresponding representation hypothesis is not only true but is the key to understanding how such systems operate. The essence of computation lies in the correspondence between the manipulation of formal tokens and the attribution of a meaning to those tokens as representing elements in worlds of some kind. Explicit concern with representation is one of the criteria often used in distinguishing artificial intelligence from other areas of computer science.

The question of knowledge and representation is central to the design of computer-based devices intended as tools for 'knowledge amplification.' We may seek to devise means of manipulating knowledge, in the sense that a word processor allows us to manipulate text. We might attempt to build systems that 'apply knowledge' towards some desired end. In this effort, our choice of problems and solutions will be strongly affected by our overall understanding of what knowledge is and how it is used. Many of the expert systems being developed in 'knowledge engineering' research are based on a straightforward acceptance of the representation hypothesis. In Chapter 10 we will describe these efforts and their limitations, and characterize the kinds of *systematic domains* that can be successfully treated in representational terms.

6.3　Pre-understanding and background

Chapter 3 emphasized that our openness to experience is grounded in a pre-understanding without which understanding itself would not be possible. An individual's pre-understanding is a result of experience within a tradition. Everything we say is said against the background of that experience and tradition, and makes sense only with respect to it. Language (as well as other meaningful actions) need express only what is not obvious, and can occur only between individuals who share to a large degree the same background. Knowledge is *always* the result of interpretation,

---

[1]This assumption, which has also been called the *physical symbol system hypothesis*, is discussed at length in Chapter 8.

which depends on the entire previous experience of the interpreter and on situatedness in a tradition. It is neither 'subjective' (particular to the individual) nor 'objective' (independent of the individual).

Maturana describes a closely related phenomenon in explaining how the previous structure of the system defines its domain of perturbations. The organism does not exist in an externally defined space. Its history of structural coupling generates a continually changing space of possible perturbations that will select among its states. Interacting systems engage in mutual structural coupling, in which the structure of each one plays a role in selecting among the perturbations (and hence the sequence of structures) of the others.

Our presentation of speech act theory has also emphasized the role of background and interpretation, while retaining a central focus on the commitment engendered by language acts. In this we move away from the individual-centered approach of looking at the mental state (intentions) of speaker and hearer, describing instead the patterns of interaction that occur within a shared background. As we will show in detail in Chapter 12, the pervasive importance of shared background has major consequences for the design of computer systems.

Artificial intelligence is an attempt to build a full account of human cognition into a formal system (a computer program). The computer operates with a background only to the extent that the background is articulated and embodied in its programs. But the articulation of the unspoken is a never-ending process. In order to describe our pre-understanding, we must do it in a language and a background that itself reflects a pre-understanding. The effort of articulation is important and useful, but it can never be complete.

This limitation on the possibility of articulation also affects more concrete issues in designing computer tools. If we begin with the implicit or explicit goal of producing an objective, background-free language for interacting with a computer system, then we must limit our domain to those areas in which the articulation can be complete (for the given purposes). This is possible, but not for the wide range of purposes to which computers are applied. Many of the problems that are popularly attributed to 'computerization' are the result of forcing our interactions into the narrow mold provided by a limited formalized domain.

At the other extreme lies the attempt to build systems that allow us to interact as though we were conversing with another person who shares our background. The result can easily be confusion and frustration, when breakdowns reveal the complex ways in which the computer fails to meet our unspoken assumptions about how we will be understood. The goal of creating computers that understand natural language must be reinterpreted (as we will argue in Chapter 9) in light of this. We must be especially careful in dealing with so-called 'expert systems.' The ideal of an objectively knowledgeable expert must be replaced with a recognition of the importance of background. This can lead to the design of tools that facilitate a dialog of evolving understanding among a knowledgeable community.

6.4   Language and action

Popular accounts of language often portray it as a means of communication by which information is passed from one person (or machine) to another. An important consequence of the critique presented in the first part of this book is that language cannot be understood as the transmission of information.

Language is a form of human social action, directed towards the creation of what Maturana calls 'mutual orientation.' This orientation is not grounded in a correspondence between language and the world, but exists as a consensual domain—as interlinked patterns of activity. The shift from language as description to language as action is the basis of speech act theory, which emphasizes the *act* of language rather than its representational role.

In our discussion of language we have particularly stressed that speech acts create commitment. In revealing commitment as the basis for language, we situate it in a social structure rather than in the mental activity of individuals. Our reason for this emphasis is to counteract the forgetfulness of commitment that pervades much of the discussion (both theoretical and commonplace) about language. The rationalistic tradition takes language as a representation—a carrier of information—and conceals its central social role. To be human is to be the kind of being that generates commitments, through speaking and listening. Without our ability to create and accept (or decline) commitments we are acting in a less than fully human way, and we are not fully using language.

This dimension is not explicitly developed in work on hermeneutics (including Heidegger) or in Maturana's account of linguistic domains. It is developed in speech act theory (especially in later work like that of Habermas) and is a crucial element in our analysis of the uses of computer technology. This key role develops from the recognition that computers are fundamentally tools for human action. Their power as tools for linguistic action derives from their ability to manipulate formal tokens of the kinds that constitute the structural elements of languages. But they are incapable of making commitments and cannot themselves enter into language.

The following chapters introduce discussions of the possibilities for 'intelligent computers,' 'computer language understanding,' 'expert systems,' and 'computer decision making.' In each case there is a pervasive misunderstanding based on the failure to recognize the role of commitment in language. For example, a computer program is not an expert, although it can be a highly sophisticated medium for communication among experts, or between an expert and someone needing help in a specialized domain. This understanding leads us to re-evaluate current research directions and suggest alternatives.

One possibility we will describe at some length in Chapter 11 is the design of tools that facilitate human communication through explicit application of speech act theory. As we pointed out in the introduction, computers are linguistic tools. On the basis of our understanding of commitment, we can create devices whose form of readiness-to-hand leads to more effective communication. We discuss a particular family of devices called 'coordination systems' that help us to recognize and create the commitment structures in our linguistic acts. In using such tools, people will be directed into a greater awareness of the social dimensions of their language and of its role in effective action.

6.5 Breakdown and the ontology of design

The preceding sections have discussed background and commitment. The third major discussion in the preceding chapters was about 'breakdown,' which is especially relevant to the question of design.

In designing new artifacts, tools, organizational structures, managerial practices, and so forth, a standard approach is to talk about 'problems' and 'problem solving.' A great deal of literature has been devoted to this topic, in a variety of disciplines. The difficulty with such an approach, which has been deeply influenced by the rationalistic tradition, is that it tends to grant problems some kind of objective existence, failing to take account of the blindness inherent in the way problems are formulated.

A 'problem' always arises for human beings in situations where they live—in other words, it arises in relation to a background. Different interpreters will see and talk about different problems requiring different tools, potential actions, and design solutions. In some cases, what is a problem for one person won't be a problem at all for someone else.

Here, as elsewhere, we want to break with the rationalistic tradition, proposing a different language for situations in which 'problems' arise. Following Heidegger, we prefer to talk about 'breakdowns.' By this we mean the interrupted moment of our habitual, standard, comfortable 'being-in-the-world .' Breakdowns serve an extremely important cognitive function, revealing to us the nature of our practices and equipment, making them 'present-to-hand' to us, perhaps for the first time. In this sense they function in a positive rather than a negative way.

New design can be created and implemented only in the space that emerges in the recurrent structure of breakdown. A design constitutes an interpretation of breakdown and a committed attempt to anticipate future breakdowns. In Chapter 10 we will discuss breakdowns in relation to the design of expert systems, and in Chapter 11 their role in management and decision making.

Most important, though, is the fundamental role of breakdown in creating the space of what can be said, and the role of language in creating our world. The key to much of what we have been saying in the preceding chapters lies in recognizing the fundamental importance of the shift from an individual-centered conception of understanding to one that is socially based. Knowledge and understanding (in both the cognitive and linguistic senses) do not result from formal operations on mental representations of an objectively existing world. Rather, they arise from the individual's committed participation in mutually oriented patterns of behavior that are embedded in a socially shared background of concerns, actions, and beliefs. This shift from an individual to a social perspective—from mental representation to patterned interaction—permits language and cognition to merge. Because of what Heidegger calls our 'thrownness,' we are largely forgetful of the social dimension of understanding and the commitment it entails. It is only when a breakdown occurs that we become aware of the fact that 'things' in our world exist not as the result of individual acts of cognition but through our active participation in a domain of discourse and mutual concern.

In this view, language—the public manifestation in speech and writing of this mutual orientation—is no longer merely a reflective but rather a constitutive medium. We create and give meaning to the world we live in and share with others. To put the point in a more radical form, we design ourselves (and the social and technological networks in which our lives have meaning) in language.

Computers do not exist, in the sense of things possessing objective features and functions, outside of language. They are created in the conversations human beings engage in when they cope with and anticipate breakdown. Our central claim in this book is that the current theoretical discourse about computers is based on a misinterpretation of the nature of human cognition and language. Computers designed on the basis of this misconception provide only impoverished possibilities for modelling and enlarging the scope of human understanding. They are restricted to representing knowledge as the acquisition and manipulation of facts, and communication as the transferring of information. As a result, we are now witnessing a major breakdown in the design of computer technology—a breakdown that reveals the rationalistically oriented background of discourse in which our current understanding is embedded.

The question we now have to deal with is how to design computers on the basis of the new discourse about language and thought that we have been elaborating. Computers are not only designed in language but are themselves equipment for language. They will not just reflect our understanding of language, but will at the same time create new possibilities for the speaking and listening that we do—for creating ourselves in language.

PART II

Computation, Thought, and Language

Chapter 7

Computers and representation

This book is directed towards understanding what can be done with computers. In Part I we developed a theoretical orientation towards human thought and language, which serves as the background for our analysis of the technological potential. In Part II we turn towards the technology itself, with particular attention to revealing the assumptions underlying its development. In this chapter we first establish a context for talking about computers and programming in general, laying out some basic issues that apply to all programs, including the artificial intelligence work that we will describe in subsequent chapters. We go into some detail here so that readers not familiar with the design of computer systems will have a clearer perspective both on the wealth of detail and on the broad relevance of a few general principles.

Many books on computers and their implications begin with a description of the formal aspects of computing, such as binary numbers, Boolean logic, and Turing machines. This sort of material is necessary for technical mastery and can be useful in dispelling the mysteries of how a machine can do computation at all. But it turns attention away from the more significant aspects of computer systems that arise from their larger-scale organization as collections of interacting components (both physical and computational) based on a formalization of some aspect of the world. In this chapter we concentrate on the fundamental issues of language and rationality that are the background for designing and programming computers.

We must keep in mind that our description is based on an idealization in which we take for granted the functioning of computer systems according to their intended design. In the actual use of computers there is a critical larger domain, in which new issues arise from the breakdowns ('bugs' and 'malfunctions') of both hardware and software. Furthermore, behind these technical aspects are the concerns of the people who design, build, and use the devices. An understanding of what a computer really does is an understanding of the social and political situation in which it is designed, built, purchased, installed, and used. Most unsuccessful computing systems have been relatively successful at the raw technical level but failed because of not dealing with breakdowns and not being designed appropriately for the context in which they were to be operated.[1]

It is beyond the scope of our book to deal thoroughly with all of these matters. Our task is to provide a theoretical orientation within which we can identify significant concerns and ask appropriate questions. In showing how programming depends on representation we are laying one cornerstone for the understanding of programs, and in particular of programs that are claimed to be intelligent.

7.1 Programming as representation

The first and most obvious point is that whenever someone writes a program, it is a program about something.[2] Whether it be the orbits of a satellite, the bills and payroll of a corporation, or the movement of spaceships on a video screen, there is some subject domain to which the programmer addresses the program.

For the moment (until we refine this view in section 7.2) we can regard the underlying machine as providing a set of storage cells, each of which can hold a *symbol structure*, either a number or a sequence of characters (letters, numerals, and punctuation marks). The steps of a program specify operations on the contents of those cells—copying them into other cells, comparing them, and modifying them (for example by adding two numbers or removing a character from a sequence).

In setting up a program, the programmer has in mind a systematic correspondence by which the contents of certain storage cells *represent* objects and relationships within the subject domain. For example, the contents of three of the cells may represent the location of some physical object with respect to a Cartesian coordinate system and unit of measurement. The operations by which these contents are modified as the program runs are designed to correspond to some desired calculation about the location of

---

[1]The nature and importance of this social embedding of computers is described by Kling and Scacchi in "The web of computing"(1982).

[2]We will ignore special cases like the construction of a sequence of instructions whose purpose is simply to exercise the machine to test it for flaws.

that object, for example in tracking a satellite. Similarly, the sequence of characters in a cell may represent the name or address of a person for whom a paycheck is being prepared.

Success in programming depends on designing a representation and set of operations that are both *veridical* and *effective*. They are veridical to the extent that they produce results that are correct relative to the domain: they give the actual location of the satellite or the legal deductions from the paycheck. They are effective to varying degrees, depending on how efficiently the computational operations can be carried out. Much of the detailed content of computer science lies in the design of representations that make it possible to carry out some class of operations efficiently.

Research on artificial intelligence has emphasized the problem of representation. In typical artificial intelligence programs, there is a more complex correspondence between what is to be represented and the corresponding form in the machine. For example, to represent the fact that the location of a particular object is "between 3 and 5 miles away" or "somewhere near the orbiter," we cannot use a simple number. There must be conventions by which some structures (e.g., sequences of characters) correspond to such facts. Straightforward mappings (such as simply storing English sentences) raise insuperable problems of effectiveness. The operations for coming to a conclusion are no longer the well-understood operations of arithmetic, but call for some kind of higher-level reasoning.

In general, artificial intelligence researchers make use of formal logical systems (such as predicate calculus) for which the available operations and their consequences are well understood. They set up correspondences between formulas in such a system and the things being represented in such a way that the operations achieve the desired veridicality. There is a great deal of argument as to the most important properties of such a formal system, but the assumptions that underlie all of the standard approaches can be summarized as follows:

1. There is a structure of formal symbols that can be manipulated according to a precisely defined and well-understood system of rules.

2. There is a mapping through which the relevant properties of the domain can be represented by symbol structures. This mapping is systematic in that a community of programmers can agree as to what a given structure represents.

3. There are operations that manipulate the symbols in such a way as to produce veridical results—to derive new structures that represent the domain in such a way that the programmers would find them accurate representations. Programs can be written that combine these operations to produce desired results.

The problem is that representation is in the mind of the beholder. There is nothing in the design of the machine or the operation of the program that depends in any way on the fact that the symbol structures are viewed as representing anything at all.[3]

There are two cases in which it is not immediately obvious that the significance of what is stored in the machine is externally attributed: the case of robot-like machines with sensors and effectors operating in the physical world, and the case of symbols with internal referents, such as those representing locations and instructions within the machine. We will discuss the significance of robots in Chapter 8, and for the moment will simply state that, for the kinds of robots that are constructed in artificial intelligence, none of the significant issues differ from those discussed here.

The problem of 'meta-reference' is more complex. Newell and Simon, in their discussion of physical symbol systems ("Computer science as an empirical inquiry," 1976), argue that one essential feature of intelligent systems is that some of the symbols can be taken as referring to operations and other symbols within the machine: not just for an outside observer, but as part of the causal mechanism.

Even in this case there is a deep and important sense in which the referential relationship is still not intrinsic. However, the arguments are complex and not central to our discussion. We are primarily concerned with how computers are used in a practical context, where the central issue is the representation of the external world. The ability of computers to coherently represent their own instructions and internal structure is an interesting and important technical consideration, but not one that affects our perspective.

7.2   Levels of representation

In the previous section, computers were described rather loosely as being able to carry out operations on symbol structures of various kinds. However this is not a direct description of their physical structure and functioning. Theoretically, one could describe the operation of a digital computer purely in terms of electrical impulses travelling through a complex network of electronic elements, without treating these impulses as symbols for anything. Just as a particular number in the computer might represent some relevant domain object (such as the location of a satellite), a deeper analysis shows that the number itself is not an object in

---

[3]This point has been raised by a number of philosophers, such as Fodor in "Methodological solipsism considered as a research strategy in cognitive psychology" (1980), and Searle in "Minds, brains, and programs" (1980). We will discuss its relevance to language understanding in Chapter 9.

the computer, but that some pattern of impulses or electrical states in turn *represents* the number. One of the properties unique to the digital computer is the possibility of constructing systems that cascade levels of representation one on top of another to great depth.

The computer programmer or theorist does not begin with a view of the computer as a physical machine with which he or she interacts, but as an abstraction—a formalism for describing patterns of behavior. In programming, we begin with a language whose individual components describe simple acts and objects. Using this language, we build up descriptions of *algorithms* for carrying out a desired task. As a programmer, one views the behavior of the system as being totally determined by the program. The language implementation is opaque in that the detailed structure of computer systems that actually carry out the task are not relevant in the domain of behavior considered by the programmer.

If we observe a computer running a typical artificial intelligence program, we can analyze its behavior at any of the following levels:

The physical machine. The machine is a complex network of components such as wires, integrated circuits, and magnetic disks. These components operate according to the laws of physics, generating patterns of electrical and magnetic activity. Of course, any understandable description will be based on finding a modular decomposition of the whole machine into components, each of which can be described in terms of its internal structure and its interaction with other components. This decomposition is recursive—a single component of one structure is in turn a composite made up of smaller structures. At the bottom of this decomposition one finds the basic physical elements, such as strands of copper and areas of semiconductor metal laid down on a wafer of silicon crystal. It is important to distinguish this kind of hierarchical decomposition into components (at a single level) from the analysis of levels of representation.

The logical machine. The computer designer does not generally begin with a concept of the machine as a collection of physical components, but as a collection of logical elements. The components at this level are logical abstractions such as or-gates, inverters, and flip-flops (or, on a higher level of the decomposition, multiplexers, arithmetic-logical units, and address decoders). These abstractions are represented by activity in the physical components. For example, certain ranges of voltages are interpreted as representing a logical 'true' and other ranges a logical 'false.' The course of changes over time is interpreted as a sequence of discrete cycles, with the activity considered stable at the end of each cycle. If the machine is properly designed, the representation at this level is veridical—patterns of activity interpreted as logic will lead to other patterns according to the rules of logic. In any real machine, at early stages of debugging, this representation will be incomplete. There will be behavior caused by phenomena such as irregular voltages and faulty synchronization that does not accurately represent the logical machine. In a properly working machine, all of the *relevant* physical behavior can be characterized in terms of the logic it represents.

The abstract machine. The logical machine is still a network of components, with activity distributed throughout. Most of today's computers are described in terms of an abstract single sequential processor, which steps through a series of instructions. It is at this level of representation that a logical pattern (a pattern of trues and falses) is interpreted as representing a higher-level symbol such as a number or a character. Each instruction is a simple operation of fetching or storing a symbol or performing a logical or arithmetic operation, such as a comparison, an addition, or a multiplication. The activity of the logical machine cannot be segmented into disjoint time slices that represent the steps of the abstract machine. In a modern machine, at any one moment the logical circuits will be simultaneously completing one step (storing away its results), carrying out the following one (e.g., doing an arithmetic operation), and beginning the next (analyzing it to see where its data are to be fetched from). Other parts of the circuitry may be performing tasks needed for the ongoing function of the machine (e.g., sending signals that prevent items from fading from memory cells), which are independent of the abstract machine steps. Most descriptions of computers are at the level of the abstract machine, since this is usually the lowest level at which the programmer has control over the details of activity.[4]

A high-level language. Most programs today are written in languages such as FORTRAN, BASIC, COBOL, and LISP, which provide elementary operations at a level more suitable for representing real-world domains. For example, a single step can convey a complex mathematical operation such as "$x = (y+z)*3/z$." A compiler or interpreter[5] converts a formula like this into a sequence of operations for the abstract machine. A higher-level language can be based on more complex symbol structures, such as lists, trees, and character strings. In LISP, for example, the contents of a number of storage cells in the underlying abstract machine can

---

[4]Even this story is too simple. It was true of computers ten years ago, but most present-day computers have an additional level called 'micro-code' which implements the abstract machine instructions in terms of instructions for a simpler abstract machine which in turn is defined in terms of the logical machine.

[5]The difference between compiling and interpretation is subtle and is not critical for our discussion.

be interpreted together as representing a list of items. To the LISP programmer, the list "(APPLES ORANGES PUDDING PIE)" is a single symbol structure to which operations such as "REVERSE" can be applied. Once again, there need be no simple correspondence between an operation at the higher level and those at the lower level that represent it. If several formulas all contain the term "(y+z)" the compiler may produce a sequence of machine steps which does the addition only once, then saves the result for use in all of the steps containing those formulas. If asked the question "Which formula is it computing right now?" the answer may not be a single high-level step.

A representation scheme for 'facts'. Programs for artificial intelligence use the symbol structures of a higher-level language to represent facts about the world. As mentioned above, there are a number of different conventions for doing this, but for any one program there must be a uniform organization. For example, an operation that a programmer would describe as "Store the fact that the person named 'Eric' lives in Chicago" may be encoded in the high-level language as a series of manipulations on a data base, or as the addition of a new proposition to a collection of axioms. There will be specific numbers or sequences of characters associated with "Eric" and "Chicago" and with the relationship "lives in." There will be a convention for organizing these to systematically represent the fact that it is Eric who lives in Chicago, not vice versa. At this level, the objects being manipulated lie once again in the domain of logic (as they did several levels below), but here instead of simple Boolean (two-valued) variables, they are formulas that stand for propositions. The relevant operators are those of logical inference, such as instantiating a general proposition for a particular individual, or using an inference rule to derive a new proposition from existing ones.

In designing a program to carry out some task, the programmer thinks in terms of the subject domain and the highest of these levels that exists for the programming system, dealing with the objects and operations it makes available. The fact that these are in turn represented at a lower level (and that in turn at a still lower one) is only of secondary relevance, as discussed in the following section. For someone designing a program or piece of hardware at one of the lower levels, the subject domain is the next higher level itself.

The exact form of this tower of levels is not critical, and may well change as new kinds of hardware are designed and as new programming concepts evolve. This detail has been presented to give some sense of the complexity that lies between an operation that a programmer would mention in describing what a program does and the operation of the physical computing device. People who have not programmed computers have not generally had experiences that provide similar intuitions about systems. One obvious fact is that for a typical complex computer program, there is no intelligible correspondence between operations at distant levels. If you ask someone to characterize the activity in the physical circuits when the program is deciding where the satellite is, there is no answer that can be given except by building up the description level by level. Furthermore, in going from level to level there is no preservation of modularity. A single high-level language step (which is chosen from many different types available) may compile into code using all of the different machine instructions, and furthermore the determination of what it compiles into will depend on global properties of the higher-level code.

7.3   Can computers do more than you tell them to do?

Readers who have had experience with computers will have noted that the story told in the previous section is too simple. It emphasizes the opacity of implementation, which is one of the key intellectual contributions of computer science. In the construction of physical systems, it is a rare exception for there to be a complete coherent level of design at which considerations of physical implementation at a lower level are irrelevant. Computer systems on the other hand can exhibit many levels of representation, each of which is understood independently of those below it. One designs an algorithm as a collection of commands for manipulating logical formulas, and can understand its behavior without any notion of how this description will be written in a higher-level language, how that program will be converted into a sequence of instructions for the abstract machine, how those will be interpreted as sequences of instructions in micro-code, how those in turn cause the switching of logic circuits, or how those are implemented using physical properties of electronic components. Theoretically, the machine as structured at any one of these levels could be replaced by a totally different one without affecting the behavior as seen at any higher level.

We have oversimplified matters, however, by saying that all of the relevant aspects of what is happening at one level can be characterized in terms of what they represent at the next higher level. This does not take into account several issues:

Breakdowns. First of all, the purely layered account above is based on the assumption that each level operates as a representation exactly as anticipated. This is rarely the case. In describing the step from electronic circuits to logic circuits, we pointed out that it took careful debugging to guarantee that the behavior of the machine could be accurately described in terms of the logic. There is a similar problem at each juncture, and a person writing a program at any one level often needs to understand (and potentially modify) how it is represented at the one below. The domain of breakdowns generated by the lower levels must be reflected in the domain for understanding the higher ones. This kind of interdependence is universally viewed as a defect in the system, and great pains are taken to avoid it, but it can never be avoided completely.

Resource use. Even assuming that a description at a higher level is adequate (the representation is veridical), there may be properties of the machine that can be described only at a lower level but which are relevant to the efficiency with which the higher-level operations are carried out. For example, two operations that are both primitive in a higher-level language may take very different amounts of time or physical storage to run on a given machine with a given *implementation* (representation of the higher-level language on the abstract machine). Although this may not be relevant in specifying what the result will be, it will be relevant to the process of getting it. In real-time systems, where the computer activates physical devices at times that have relevance in the subject domain (e.g., a controller for an industrial process, or a collision avoidance system for aircraft), the speed of execution may be critical. In the use of storage, there are often limits on how much can be stored, and the details of when these limits will be reached can be described only on the lower levels.

Differing attitudes are taken to cross-level dependencies that deal with resources. Some programmers argue that whenever resources are significant, the program should be written at the level where they can be directly described, rather than a higher level. For example they argue that real-time control processes should be written in assembly language (a language that corresponds closely to the abstract machine) rather than in a higher-level language, since the resources connected with the objects and operations of the abstract machine can be directly specified. Others argue that the program should be designed at the higher level only, and that the lower-level systems should provide higher-level operations that are so efficient that there never need be a concern. In practice, programs are often initially designed without taking into account the lower level, and then modified to improve performance.

Accidental representation. There are some cases in which there are useful higher-level descriptions of a program's behavior that do not correspond to an intentional representation by a programmer. As a simple example, there have been a number of 'display hack' programs that produce geometrical designs on a computer screen. Many of these grew out of programs that were originally created to perform operations on symbols that had nothing to do with visual figures. When the contents of some of their internal storage cells were interpreted as numbers representing points on a video display screen, strikingly regular patterns emerged, which the programmer had not anticipated. One such program produces figures containing circular forms and might be appropriately described as "drawing a circle," even though the concept of circle did not play a role in the design of its mechanisms at any level. In these cases, the description of the program as representing something is a description by some observer after the fact, rather than by its designer.

If it were not for this last possibility we could argue that any properly constructed computer program is related to a subject domain only through the relationships of representation intended by its programmers. However there remains the logical possibility that a computer could end up operating successfully within a domain totally unintended by its designers or the programmers who constructed its programs.

This possibility is related to the issues of structural coupling and instructional interaction raised by Maturana. He argues that structures in the nervous system do not represent the world in which the organism lives. Similarly one could say of the display hack program that its structures do not represent the geometrical objects that it draws. It is possible that we might (either accidentally or intentionally) endow a machine with essential qualities we do not anticipate. In Section 8.4 we will discuss the relevance of this observation to the question of whether computers can think.

Chapter 8

Computation and intelligence

Questions concerning the future uses of computers are often intertwined with questions about whether they will be intelligent. The existence of a field called 'artificial intelligence' implies that possibility and, as we pointed out in our introduction, there have been many speculations on the social impact of such developments. The theoretical principles developed in the earlier chapters lead us to the conclusion that one cannot program computers to be intelligent and that we need to look in different directions for the design of powerful computer technology. Our goal in this chapter is to ground that conclusion in an analysis and critique of claims about artificial intelligence. We begin by examining the background in which the question of machine intelligence has been raised.

8.1   Why do we ask?

The first question one might ask is why anyone would consider that computers *could* be intelligent. A computer, like a clock or an adding machine, is a complex physical device exhibiting patterns of activity that represent some external world. But it hardly seems worthwhile asking whether a clock or an adding machine is intelligent. What then is different about computers?

There is no simple answer to this question—no sharp distinction that clearly separates clocks from computers and puts the latter into a class of potential thinkers. The differences are all differences of degree (albeit large ones), along a number of dimensions:

Apparent autonomy. It has been argued that the clock played a major role in the development of our understanding of physical systems because it exhibited a kind of autonomy that is not shared by most mechanical tools. Although it is built for a purpose, once it is running it can go on for a long time (even indefinitely) without any need for human intervention. This feature of autonomous operation made it possible for the clock to provide a model for aspects of the physical world, such as the motions of the planets, and of biological organisms as well. The computer exhibits this kind of autonomy to a much larger degree. Once it has been programmed it can carry out complex sequences of operations without human intervention.

Complexity of purpose. A clock may be complex in the details of its construction, but its overall structure is determined by a clear, understandable purpose. All of the parts and their activities can be explained in terms of their contribution to the regular rotation of the hands. The complexity can be broken down in a modular way. A computer system, on the other hand, need not have a single purpose. The activities of a large modern time-sharing system can be understood only by looking at the entire range of services provided for users. There is no way to assign a single global purpose to any one detail of its construction or operation. Each detail may be the result of an evolved compromise between many conflicting demands. At times, the only explanation for the system's current form may be an appeal to this history of modification.

Structural plasticity. Most physical mechanisms (including clocks) do not undergo structural change over time. Their dynamic changes (the motion of the parts) leave the basic structure constant. Computer systems, on the other hand, can undergo continual structural change. Every time a program is run, a file written, or a new program added, the system (viewed at the appropriate level) undergoes a change that may cause it to act differently in the future. In Maturana's terms, machines such as clocks only undergo structural changes of first order: changes in relations between components with properties that remain invariant. Computers and other such systems also undergo structural changes of second order: changes in the properties of components that are themselves composite unities. As discussed in Chapter 7, an account of the system as having changed will generally be at one of the higher (software) levels. From the point of view of the hardware, the structural relationships (as opposed to the state) of the computer don't change any more than a radio changes depending on the station it is tuned to. One of the powers of the layering described in Chapter 7 is the potential for building mutable higher-level structure (which determines behavior) on a relatively fixed underlying physical structure.

Unpredictability. As a consequence of complexity and plasticity, the activity of a computer (even when running without errors) is often unpredictable in an important sense. Of course, it is predictable at the physical level—a complete simulation of the machine executing the program would lead to predictions of the same results. But this is like saying that the activity of an organism is predictable by carrying out a simulation of its physical cells. The simulation is of an order of complexity that makes it uninteresting as a predictive mechanism. Similarly, in a complex computer system designed and functioning properly at a higher level there is often no way to predict how a program will act, short of running it (or simulating it step by step, which is of the same complexity). In interacting with such a system we tend to treat it in the same way we treat organisms—we operate by perturbing it and observing the results, gradually building up an understanding of its behavior.

The net effect of these quantitative differences is to create an apparent qualitative leap, from the 'ordinary' properties of adding machines and clocks to the 'mind-like' qualities of the computer. It is important to note that the differences do not result from the fact that computers use symbols (so do adding machines, to the same extent) or that they contain general purpose processors (so do many current microwave ovens). The differences result from global properties of the overall systems within which computers function.

8.2 Intelligence as rational problem solving

Chapter 2 described how artificial intelligence developed out of attempts to formalize problem-solving behavior, under the influence of Simon's work on rational decision making. A problem or task is analyzed in terms of a 'problem space,' generated by a finite set of properties and operations. A 'solution' is a particular point in that space that has the desired properties. Problem solving is a process of search for a sequence of operations that will lead to a solution point. Although this model was initially applied in a very direct sense in the design of programs such as GPS (the General Problem Solver[1]), it can be applied in a more general sense to most work in artificial intelligence.

We can begin to grasp the limitations of this approach to intelligence by looking carefully at what must go on when someone constructs a computer program. Several distinct tasks need to be carried out (although not necessarily in isolation of one another, or in the particular order given here). They may at times be assigned to different people, with job titles

---

[1]See Newell and Simon, *Human Problem Solving* (1972).

such as 'system analyst,' 'knowledge engineer,' and 'programmer.' For simplicity we will refer to a single 'programmer.'

1. **Characterizing the task environment.** First, the programmer must have a clear analysis of just what constitutes the task and the potential set of actions for the program. The task cannot be described with some vague generality like "diagnose illnesses" or "understand newspaper stories" but must be precisely stated in terms of the relevant *objects* of the environment and the particular *properties* that are to be considered. As we will discuss at length later, this task is the most critical. It results in the generation of a *systematic domain*, which embodies the programmer's interpretation of the situation in which the program will function.

2. **Designing a formal representation.** A major constraint on the characterization of the task environment is the need for a formal symbolic representation in which everything relevant can be stated explicitly. This formal representation may not look like mathematical logic, but it does need to be formal in that fully explicit rules can be set down for just what constitutes a well-formed representation, and in that it must be manipulable in ways that correspond to the task environment. One of the major activities in theoretical artificial intelligence has been the attempt to design formal systems that can adequately and consistently represent facts about the world.

3. **Embodying the representation in the computer system.** A formal representation is an abstraction. In order to use it in building a computer system, we need to set its structures in correspondence with the structures available on the computer at some level. A particular formal representation may be embodied in many different ways, each having different properties with regard to the computations that can be carried out. The critical thing is that the embodiment remain faithful to the formal system—that the operations carried out by the computer system are consistent with the rules of the formal system.[2]

4. **Implementing a search procedure.** Finally, the programmer designs a procedure that operates on the embodied representation

---

[2]Practitioners of artificial intelligence will be aware that in many cases the programmer deals directly with the correspondence between the subject domain and the symbol structures provided by a higher-level programming language, with no systematic level of logical representation. It is coming to be widely accepted (see, for example, Hayes, "In defence of logic," 1977; Nilsson, *Principles of Artificial Intelligence,* 1980; Newell, "The knowledge level," 1982) that this kind of haphazard formal system cannot be used to build comprehensible programs, and that the distinction between the logical formalism and its embodiment in a computation is critical.

structures in order to carry out the desired task. As mentioned above, the procedure may or may not be directly characterized as search. Its critical property is its faithfulness to the formal system, whether that system is mathematical logic, procedural reasoning, fuzzy logic, pattern matching, or other such systems. For each of these there are underlying formal rules that, though they may differ from standard deductive logic, nevertheless determine what constitutes a valid representation and what can be done with it. Without a precise understanding of these rules, there would be no way to design a computer program.

8.3   The phenomenon of blindness

The summary in the previous section prepares us to look at the question of machine intelligence in relation to Heidegger's account of 'blindness.' As we discussed in Chapter 3, Heidegger argues that the basis for an understanding of cognition is *being-in-the-world*. Our ability to treat our experience as involving *present-at-hand* objects and properties is derived from a pre-conscious experience of them as *ready-to-hand*. The essence of our Being is the pre-reflective experience of being *thrown* in a situation of acting, without the opportunity or need to disengage and function as detached observers. Reflection and abstraction are important phenomena, but are not the basis for our everyday action.

Whenever we treat a situation as present-at-hand, analyzing it in terms of objects and their properties, we thereby create a blindness. Our view is limited to what can be expressed in the terms we have adopted. This is not a flaw to be avoided in thinking—on the contrary, it is necessary and inescapable. Reflective thought is impossible without the kind of abstraction that produces blindness. Nevertheless we must be aware of the limitations that are imposed.

In writing a computer program, the programmer is responsible for characterizing the task domain as a collection of objects, properties, and operations, and for formulating the task as a structure of goals in terms of these. Obviously, this is not a matter of totally free choice. The programmer acts within a context of language, culture, and previous understanding, both shared and personal. The program is forever limited to working within the world determined by the programmer's explicit articulation of possible objects, properties, and relations among them. It therefore embodies the blindness that goes with this articulation.

There are restricted task domains in which this blindness does not preclude behavior that appears intelligent. For example, many games are amenable to a direct application of the techniques described in the previous section to produce a program that outplays human opponents. There is no *a priori* reason to doubt that this will be true even for highly complex games such as chess. There are also domains where so-called 'expert systems' can be built successfully, such as the manipulation of algebraic expressions, the analysis of chemical spectrograms, and the recognition of anomalies in electrocardiograms. As with games, these are areas in which the identification of the relevant features is straightforward and the nature of solutions is clearcut.

If we look at intelligence in a broader context, however, the inadequacies of a program with built-in permanent blindness begin to emerge. The essence of intelligence is to act appropriately when there is no simple pre-definition of the problem or the space of states in which to search for a solution. Rational search within a problem space is not possible until the space itself has been created, and is useful only to the extent that the formal structure corresponds effectively to the situation.

It should be no surprise, then, that the area in which artificial intelligence has had the greatest difficulty is in the programming of common sense. It has long been recognized that it is much easier to write a program to carry out abstruse formal operations than to capture the common sense of a dog. This is an obvious consequence of Heidegger's realization that it is precisely in our 'ordinary everydayness' that we are immersed in readiness-to-hand. A methodology by which formally defined tasks can be performed with carefully designed representations (making things present-at-hand) does not touch on the problem of blindness. We accuse people of lacking common sense precisely when some representation of the situation has blinded them to a space of potentially relevant actions.

There has been a certain amount of discussion in the artificial intelligence literature about the possibility of a program switching between different representations, or creating new representations. If this were possible, the blindness inherent in any one representation could be overcome. But if we look carefully at what is actually proposed, it does not really confront the issues. In some cases the programmer builds in a small number of different characterizations (instead of just one), and the program is able to switch among these. In others, the so-called creation of representations does not deal at all with the characterization of the environment (which is where the problem arises), but simply with the details of the formal structures by which it is represented. In either case, the problem of blindness as created by the initial programming is untouched.

In current artificial intelligence research it is often stated that the key problem is 'knowledge acquisition.' Researchers seek to build tools that enable experts in a task domain (such as medical diagnosis) to pass their expert knowledge to a computer system. It should be apparent from the preceding discussion that this is an unreachable goal. It has generally been assumed that the difficulty of getting experts to make their knowledge explicit is one of communication—that the appropriate representation is somehow there in the expert's mind, but not accessible to introspection or verbalization. If we take the work of Heidegger and Maturana seriously, we see that experts do not need to have formalized representations in order to act.[3] They may at times manipulate representations as one part of successful activity, but it is fruitless to search for a full formalization of the pre-understanding that underlies all thought and action. As Gadamer points out, we can never have a full explicit awareness of our prejudices. This is an essential condition of human thought and language, not a failure of communication tools.

But, one might be tempted to argue, aren't we being too hasty in precluding machines from being intelligent because of their blindness? Might we not be committing the 'superhuman-human fallacy,' denying intelligence to ordinary human thought as well?

The answer to this objection was laid out in the earlier chapters. Heidegger demonstrates that the essence of our intelligence is in our thrownness, not our reflection. Similarly, Maturana shows that biological cognitive systems do not operate by manipulating representations of an external world. It is the observer who describes an activity as representing something else. Human cognition includes the use of representations, but is not based on representation. When we accept (knowingly or unknowingly) the limitations imposed by a particular characterization of the world in terms of objects and properties, we do so only provisionally. There always remains the possibility of rejecting, restructuring, and transcending that particular blindness. This possibility is not under our control—the breakdown of a representation and jump to a new one happens independently of our will, as part of our coupling to the world we inhabit.

In debates concerning the possibility of artificial intelligence, a recurrent theme has been the deriding of the common objection that machines can do only what they are told to do. Evans (*The Micro Millennium*, 1979, p. 157) gives a typical response. When asked "Surely it can only do what you have previously programmed it to do?" he suggests the answer is unexpectedly simple: "The same is true of animals and humans." It should be clear that in this response (as in all similar responses) there is a failure to distinguish between two very different things: structure-determined systems (which include people, computers, and anything else operating according to physical laws), and systems programmed explicitly with a chosen representation. Stating matters carefully: "An animal or human can do only what its structure as previously established will allow

---

[3]Dreyfus and Dreyfus, in *Mind Over Machine* (1985), argue along lines very similar to ours that expertise cannot be captured in any collection of formal rules.

it to do." But this is not at all the same as "what you have previously programmed it to do" for any "you" and any notion of "programmed" that corresponds to the way computers are actually programmed.

8.4   What about learning and evolution?

Having followed the argument this far, the reader might be tempted to object to the way we have linked the questions "Can computers be intelligent?" and "Can we construct an intelligent machine?" We have focussed on the problems of construction, showing that the requirements on the programmer lead to inevitable limitations. But what if the programmer didn't have to explicitly determine the representation and its embodiment? What if somehow these could develop on their own?

Ever since the beginning of artificial intelligence, there have been critics who have felt that the essence of intelligence lay in the ability of an organism to learn from experience, dooming any efforts to create intelligent machines by programming them. There have been many attempts to build learning programs, which begin with a minimum of structure and develop further structure either through a process of reinforcement modelled on behaviorist theories of reward and punishment or through a kind of selection modelled after theories of evolution. Recently there has been a resurgence of interest in learning programs, even among writers such as Minsky, who were sharply critical of earlier efforts.[4]

If we examine the artificial intelligence literature on learning, we find three somewhat different approaches:

Parameter adjustment. The simplest approach (and the one that has led to the most publicized results) is to limit the program's learning capacities to the adjustment of parameters that operate within a fixed representation. For example, Samuel's checker-playing program[5] contained a collection of evaluation functions, which computed the benefits of a proposed position. These functions (such as adding up the number of pieces, or seeing how many jumps were possible) gave different results for different situations. The obvious problem was deciding how much weight to give each one in the overall choice of a move. Samuel's program gradually shifted the weights and then adopted the modified weighting if the moves thereby chosen were successful.

More sophisticated applications of this technique have been developed, but the general idea remains the same: a fixed structure is in place, and

---

[4]See Minsky, "K-lines: A theory of memory" (1981).

[5]Samuel, "Some studies in machine learning using the game of checkers" (1963).

the learning consists of adjusting some kind of weights to achieve a higher
measure of performance. Although there may be some kinds of programming tasks for which this technique is useful, it clearly does not avoid
the problem of blindness, since it provides only a slight adjustment on a
preprogrammed representation.

Combinatorial concept formation. The second kind of learning program does what has been called 'concept formation' or 'concept learning.'
This approach (which has also been the source of many experiments in cognitive psychology) is motivated by the observation that people can learn to
group related objects into categories. It appears that people have a 'concept' of "horse" that enables them to distinguish horses from non-horses.
The question is how such concepts arise, since in most cases they are not
taught explicitly but are learned through experiences in which specific
objects are labelled as members or non-members of the class.

In the computer programs (and in most of the psychological experiments as well) the problem is initially characterized in terms of a set of
objects and properties, just as in the standard programming methodology
described above. For example, in Winston's program dealing with the
'blocks world,'[6] the initial formulation includes undecomposable objects
(the individual blocks) and properties (such as their color, shape, and
orientation, and whether or not they are touching). The program then
tries to find structural combinations of objects and properties that correspond to the assignment (by the programmer) of examples to categories.
Winston's program, for instance, produces the combination that we could
describe as "two vertical blocks, not abutting, with a third horizontal object supported by both of them" for the concept of "Arch" as embodied
in a specific sequence of examples. Other programs have more elaborate
mechanisms, but there is a common basis: the programmer begins by creating a representation, and the 'learning' consists of finding (and storing
for later use) combinations of its elements that satisfy some criterion.

The limitations of this approach are not as immediately obvious as
those of simple parameter adjustment, but follow directly from the discussion in the previous section. No amount of rearrangement and recombi-
nation of existing elements will ever transcend the assumptions made in
representing those elements. In general, programs of this sort have dealt
with only the simplest kinds of examples, and with 'concepts' lacking in
naturalness and generality. In order for the search for combinations to
have any chance of success at all, the initial representation must be pared
down to a small number of carefully chosen properties that will turn out

---

[6]Winston, "Learning structural descriptions from examples" (1975).

to be relevant. As Winston cautiously observes:[7] "The small number of properties associated with each object may be a cause for some uneasiness. Is it possible that the examples work only because of the careful arrangements of the slots and their small number? Maybe. Indeed one important question to be addressed as the work goes on is that of how much complexity can be coped with before the system breaks down."

Evolution of structure. The third and most ambitious kind of learning is that in which the initial system does not have a structure directly related to the task as seen by its designer. The learning machines of the early 1960s[8] and attempts at 'artificial evolution' (such as Fogel, Owens, and Walsh, *Artificial Intelligence Through Simulated Evolution*, 1966) fall into this group. In these programs the techniques of the previous two classes are applied at a microscopic level. Parameter adjustment or combinatorial search is applied, but at the level of individual elements connected in an overall web whose structure was not designed as a representation. It was hoped that a device designed on general principles (often by analogy with simple models of the nervous system) could learn a wide range of behaviors as a result of its structural coupling in a series of learning trials.

This approach is compatible with Maturana's view of structural coupling. We get a very different perspective on computers if, instead of looking at the problem of programming them, we look at them as plastic structure-determined systems. A computer system need not have a fixed structure built by a programmer but can be an evolving structure shaped by interactions. Many of the characteristics of autopoietic systems will hold for any system whose internal structure can change as a result of perturbations, and computer programs share this quality.

The evolutionary approach to artificial intelligence is theoretically possible but there has been essentially no success in getting it to work. The techniques devised for structural change at the microscopic level and the organizational structures for the connectivity of elements have been inadequate to get even the most rudimentary interesting behavior.[9] After a brief heyday in the 1950s and early 1960s, work of this sort was almost completely abandoned, to be replaced with the style of artificial intelligence research we have been describing.

This failure is not surprising if we look at the assumptions made by those who tried it. They assumed that the underlying system had a relatively simple structure, and that its complexity came from large numbers

---

[7] Winston, "Learning by creating and justifying transfer frames" (1978), p. 166.

[8] See Nilsson, *Learning Machines* (1965), for a good general introduction.

[9] "The Chaostron," by Cadwallader-Cohen, Zysiczk, and Donnelly (1961), is a satirical critique of the naivete that was evident in some of the early attempts.

of learned interconnections. The guiding image was that of a large number of essentially uniform neurons with widespread and essentially uniform potential for interconnections. Work over the years in neuroanatomy and neurophysiology has demonstrated that living organisms do not fit this image. Even an organism as small as a worm with a few hundred neurons is highly structured, and much of its behavior is the result of built-in structure, not learning.

Of course, the structure of nervous systems came into being through evolution. But if we try to duplicate evolution rather than the structural change that takes place in the lifetime of an individual, we are faced with even less knowledge of the mechanisms of change. This remains true despite recent advances in molecular genetics, which further reveal the complexity of layer upon layer of mechanisms involved at even the most microscopic level. There is also the obvious fact that the time scale of biological evolution is epochal; changes occur as a result of coupling over millions of years.

In discussions of artificial evolution it is sometimes argued that there is no need for an artificial system to evolve at this slow pace, since its internal operations are so much faster than those of organic nervous systems. Millions upon millions of 'generations' could be produced in a single day. But this is wrong for two reasons. First, nature does not do things sequentially. Although each generation for a higher organism takes days or years, there are millions of individual organisms all undergoing the process simultaneously. This high degree of parallelism more than cancels out the additional speed of computing. Second, and more important, the view that evolution can go at the speed of the machine ignores the fundamental process of structural coupling. In order for changes to be relevant to survival in the medium the organism inhabits, there must be sufficient time for those changes to have an effect on how the organism functions. The evolutionary cycle must go at the speed of the coupling, not the speed at which internal changes occur. Unless we reduce our notion of the medium to those things that can be rapidly computed (in which case we fall into all of the problems discussed above for small simplistic representations), an artificial system can evolve no faster than any other system that must undergo the same coupling.

It is highly unlikely that any system we can build will be able to undergo the kind of evolutionary change (or learning) that would enable it to come close to the intelligence of even a small worm, much less that of a person.

The issue of structural change is also closely tied to the problem of the physical embodiment of computers as robots. It has been argued that the representation relation between a computer and the world its structures describe will be different when we can build robots with visual, tactile, and other sensors and motor effectors operating in the physical domain. As a number of philosophers have pointed out,[10] a computer attached to a television camera is no different in principle from one attached to a teletype. The relevant properties and their representation are fixed by the design of the equipment. A scanned-in video scene that has been processed into an array of numerical 'pixels' (picture elements) is exactly equivalent to a long list of sentences, each of the form "The amount of light hitting the retina at point [x, y] is z."

In designing a fixed correspondence between parameters of the receptors (or effectors) and elements of the representation, the programmer is embodying exactly the sort of blindness about which we have been speaking. Once again, this does not apply to systems that, rather than being designed to implement a particular representation, evolve through structural coupling. However, the possibilities for computers whose physical structure evolves in this way are even more remote than those of programming by evolutionary change.

8.5   Can pigs have wings?

Readers well trained in the analytic tradition will by this point have concluded that our argument that computers cannot be intelligent has several 'logical holes' in it:

1. First of all, we have not given a precise definition of intelligence. The discussion of Heidegger has suggested various qualities of human intelligence but does not give the kind of clear criteria that would be needed to design objective experiments to determine whether a given system was intelligent.

2. We have explicitly said that computers can perform some tasks (such as playing complex games) as well as people: Some researchers would take this as constituting intelligent behavior. How, then, do we exclude this behavior from the domain of intelligence?

3. Finally, we have left open the possibility that some suitably designed machine or sequence of machines might be able to undergo adequate structural coupling, and hence have the same claims to intelligence as any organism, including a person. Since we accept the view that a person is a physical structure-determined system, we cannot be sure that a similar system made out of silicon and metals might not be equivalent to one composed of protoplasm.

---

[10]See, for example, Searle, "Minds, brains, and programs," 1980.

In light of these points, aren't we being illogical or inconsistent in our assertion that computers cannot be intelligent?

In order to respond to this challenge, we need to recall the theory of language developed in Chapter 5. Sentences in a human language cannot be treated as statements of fact about an objective world, but are actions in a space of commitments. If this applies to the question "Is there any water in the refrigerator?" it must apply at least as strongly to "Can computers be intelligent?"

If we assume that the person asking the question is serious, there is an underlying background of purposes and understanding (the 'horizon' as Gadamer calls it) into which the question fits. If a questioner were to ask "Can pigs have wings?" a respondent within the analytic tradition might have difficulty answering, because although the idea is outrageously farfetched, current work in genetic engineering does leave open the logical possibility of creating a beast with the desired characteristics. Admittedly, there might be some refuge in challenging the asker as to whether such a monstrosity would still properly be called a pig,[11] thereby invalidating the question. But if the question were asked seriously, neither the logical possibility nor the precise meaning of "pig" would be the issue at hand. The questioner would be asking for some reason in some background of understanding and purpose, and the appropriate answer (just like the appropriate answer to "Is there water in the refrigerator?") would have to be relevant to that background.

The background for serious questions about computer intelligence is the development of computer systems and their use in human contexts. What then is the basis for deciding whether it is appropriate to describe computers as potentially intelligent? In applying a predicate to an entity, one is implicitly committed to the belief that the entity is the kind of thing to which the predicate properly applies. In uttering a sentence containing mental terms ('intelligent,' 'perceive,' 'learn'), we are adopting an orientation towards the thing referred to by the subject of the sentence as an autonomous agent. The issue is not whether it really is autonomous—the question of free will has been debated for centuries and work in artificial intelligence has provided no new solutions. Rather, in using mental terms we commit ourselves to an orientation towards it as an autonomous agent.

There are many reasons why one can feel uncomfortable with the tendency to adopt the same orientation towards people (whom we take as autonomous beings) and towards machines. It is not a matter of being right or wrong, accurate or inaccurate, but rather of a pre-understanding that guides our discourse and our actions.

---

[11] See, for example Putnam's discussion of natural kinds in "Is semantics possible?" (1970).

In attributing intelligence to machines, one is doing more than just taking what Dennett, in "Mechanism and responsibility" (1973, p. 246), calls the 'intentional stance.' He argues that in taking an intentional stance towards computers, all one is claiming is that "on occasion, a purely physical system can be so complex, and yet so organized, that we find it convenient, explanatory, pragmatically necessary for prediction, to treat it as if it has beliefs and desires and was rational." But treating a system as though it were rational (in the formalized sense of rationality) is very different from treating it as though it had beliefs and desires, and this is a significant confusion.

We treat other people not as merely 'rational beings' but as 'responsible beings.' An essential part of being human is the ability to enter into commitments and to be responsible for the courses of action that they anticipate. A computer can never enter into a commitment (although it can be a medium in which the commitments of its designers are conveyed), and can never enter as a participant into the domain of human discourse. Our earlier chapters point out the centrality of commitment for those aspects of intelligent behavior that initially seem based on more objective ideals of rationality. Even the ability to utter a 'true statement' emerges from the potential for commitment, and the absence of this potential gives computers a wholly different kind of being.

We do not treat the question of whether computers can be intelligent as a pure stance, with one or another choice to be taken for the sake of argument. We exist within a discourse, which both prefigures and is constituted by our utterances. The meaning of any question or statement lies in its role within this discourse. Our answer to the question of whether machines can be intelligent must be understood in the context of the questions raised by the other chapters, and in the orientation that these questions provide for action.

Chapter 9

Understanding language

There is an intimate connection between intelligence and language. Many of the representation techniques described in the previous chapters were first developed in trying to process natural language[1] with computers. Our position, in accord with the preceding chapters, is that computers cannot understand language. Some important observations can be made along the route to that conclusion, and in this chapter we review the existing research work in some detail. We are concerned with the technical details here because natural language research has been the context for many of the efforts within artificial intelligence to deal with the theoretical issues we raise. Mechanisms such as 'frames,' 'scripts,' and 'resource-limited reasoning' have been proposed as ways to build machines that in some sense deal with 'understanding' and 'interpretation.' We need to examine them carefully to evaluate these claims.

9.1 Artificial intelligence and language understanding

In the mid 1960s, natural language research with computers proceeded in the wake of widespread disillusionment caused by the failure of the highly touted and heavily funded machine translation projects. There was a feeling that researchers had failed to make good on their early confident claims and that computers might not be able to deal with the complexities of human language at all. Artificial intelligence researchers took a new approach, going beyond the syntactic word-shuffling that dominated

---

[1] In discussions of computers and formal systems, the term 'natural language' is used for ordinary human languages, to distinguish them from constructed formal languages, such as the predicate calculus and FORTRAN.

machine translation. It was clear that for effective machine processing of language—whether for translation, question answering, or sophisticated information retrieval—an analysis of the syntactic structures and identification of the lexical items was not sufficient. Programs had to deal somehow with what the words and sentences *meant*.

A number of programs in this new vein were described in the early collections of papers on artificial intelligence.[2] Each program worked in some very limited domain (such as baseball scores, family trees, or algebra word problems) within which it was possible to set up formal representation structures corresponding to the meanings of sentences. These structures could be used in a systematic reasoning process as a partial simulation of language comprehension. The model of language understanding implicit in those programs (and most such programs since) rests on some basic assumptions about language and representation that we have elaborated in our earlier accounts of the rationalistic tradition:

1. Sentences in a natural language correspond to facts about the world.

2. It is possible to create a formal representation system such that:

    (a) For any relevant fact about the world there can be a corresponding structure in the representation system.

    (b) There is a systematic way of correlating sentences in natural language with structures in the representation system, so that the corresponding structure states the same fact as the sentence.

    (c) Systematic formal operations on representation structures can be devised to carry out valid reasoning.

This somewhat simplistic formulation needs elaboration to be comprehensive. It is clear, for example, that a question or command does not correspond to facts in the same manner as a statement, and that a reasoning system based on pure logic is unlikely to be sufficient. We will discuss some of these elaborations later, but for a preliminary understanding they do not play a major role.

The critical element in this approach is the systematic manipulation of a formal representation. Operations carried out on the representation structures are justified not by facts about language, but by the correspondence between the representation and the world being described. It is in this sense that such programs are said to 'understand' the words and sentences they deal with, while the earlier machine translation programs (or

---

[2]Feigenbaum and Feldman, *Computers and Thought* (1963); Minsky, *Semantic Information Processing* (1967).

other programs that deal with text using key-word recognition or statistical methods) only 'manipulate without understanding.'

Many claims have been made that the 'artificial intelligence paradigm' is new and superior to older philosophical approaches to language. But with a few notable exceptions (discussed later), these claims have proved rather empty. Fodor, in "Methodological solipsism considered as a research strategy in cognitive psychology" (1980), has pointed out that to the extent that they are clearly defined, artificial intelligence models are generally equivalent to older philosophical ones in the analytic tradition, drawing on ideas that go back to Aristotle and beyond. Before pursuing the limitations of this tradition, let us look at what has been achieved.

One of the most widely known programs of the kind described here was Winograd's SHRDLU (*Understanding Natural Language*, 1972). The program carried on a dialog with a person (via teletype) concerning the activity of a simulated robot arm in a tabletop world of toy objects (often referred to as the 'blocks world'). The program could answer questions, carry out commands, and incorporate new facts about its world. It displayed the simulated world on a video screen, showing the activities it carried out as it moved the objects around. The following dialog[3] illustrates some of its abilities (lines in lower case are typed by the person, those in upper case by the computer):

- pick up a big red block.

  OK.

- grasp the pyramid.

  I DON'T UNDERSTAND WHICH PYRAMID YOU MEAN.

- find a block which is taller than the one you are holding and put it into the box.

  OK

  . . .

- what does the box contain?

  THE BLUE PYRAMID AND THE BLUE BLOCK.

- what is the pyramid supported by?

  THE BOX.

- how many blocks are not in the box?

  FOUR OF THEM.

---

[3]Reprinted from Winograd, *Understanding Natural Language* (1972), pp. 8-15.

- is at least one of them narrower than the one which I told you to pick up?

  YES, THE RED CUBE.

- is it supported?

  YES, BY THE TABLE.

- can the table pick up blocks?

  NO.

  . . .

- had you touched any pyramid before you put the green one on the little cube?

  YES, THE GREEN ONE.

- when did you pick it up?

  WHILE I WAS STACKING UP THE RED CUBE, A LARGE RED BLOCK AND A LARGE GREEN CUBE.

- why?

  TO GET RID OF IT.

  . . .

In addition to giving responses that call for reasoning about the domain (the world of toy blocks), the system draws conclusions about the structure of the conversation and about the hypothesized knowledge of the other participant. In order to analyze a phrase like "the pyramid," context must be considered. The command "Grasp the pyramid" near the beginning of the dialog is underspecified since there are several pyramids in the robot's world. But the later question "What is the pyramid supported by?" is understood as referring to the specific pyramid mentioned in a previous response. By keeping a record of the conversation, SHRDLU could often determine the referent of a phrase. It also kept track of part of the knowledge implicit in the person's utterances, for example the fact that a particular block was referred to using its color. It could then use this to help in choosing among alternative interpretations. For example, if a block had been referred to by the person as "the green block," it would not be considered as a likely referent for "it" in a subsequent question "What color is it?"

In SHRDLU, this reasoning about the conversation did not make use of the same representation formalism as for the blocks world itself, but was done in an *ad hoc* style. Nevertheless, in essence it was no different from any other reasoning process carried out on representation structures. Later programs have refined and extended the approach, within the same theoretical background.

9.2   The problem of background

The rationalistic approach to meaning that underlies systems like SHRDLU is founded on the assumption that the meanings of words and of the sentences and phrases made up of them can be characterized independently of the interpretation given by individuals in a situation. There are, of course, aspects of meaning that call for qualifying this assumption. A sentence may include indexicals (words like "I," "you," and "now") whose referents are elements of the conversation situation, or may have connotative effects (as in the impact of a poetic metaphor) that depend on the full understanding and empathy of the hearer. But these are seen as add-ons to a central core of meaning that is context-independent. Even those who are critical of artificial intelligence are prone to accept this separation of the 'literal meaning' from other linguistic effects. Weizenbaum, for instance, argues against the possibility of computer understanding in this way:

> It may be possible... to construct a conceptual structure that corresponds to the meaning of the sentence, "Will you come to dinner with me this evening?" But it is hard to see... how [such] schemes could possibly understand that same sentence to mean a shy young man's desperate longing for love. — Weizenbaum, *Computer Power and Human Reason* (1976), p. 200.

In his review of Weizenbaum's book, McCarthy responds by pointing out that there are different kinds of understanding and by suggesting that we might expect a computer to understand literal meaning even if it were not open to the connotations and emotional subtleties of full meaning:

> This good example raises interesting issues and seems to call for some distinctions. Full understanding of the sentence indeed results in knowing about the young man's desire for love, but it would seem that there is a useful lesser level of understanding in which the machine would know only that he would like her to come to dinner. — McCarthy, "An unreasonable book" (1976), p. 86.

But as we saw in Chapters 3 and 5, the concept of literal meaning is inadequate even in dealing with the most mundane examples. The phenomena of background and interpretation pervade our everyday life. Meaning always derives from an interpretation that is rooted in a situation:

> ... relativity to situation and opportunity constitutes the very
> essence of speaking. For no statement simply has an unambigu-
> ous meaning based on its linguistic and logical construction, as
> such, but on the contrary, each is motivated. A question is be-
> hind each statement that first gives it its meaning. — Gadamer,
> *Philosophical Hermeneutics* (1976), pp. 88-89.

Gadamer, Heidegger, Habermas, and others argue that the goal of reducing even 'literal' meanings to truth conditions is ultimately impossible,
and inevitably misleading. It focusses attention on those aspects of language (such as the statement of mathematical truths) that are secondary
and derivative, while ignoring the central problems of meaning and communication. When we squeeze out the role of interpretation, we are left
not with the essence of meaning, but with the shell. Chapter 5 showed
how the meaning of a concrete term like "water" could be understood only
relative to purpose and background. Looking at computer programs, we
see this kind of problem lurking at every turn. In order for a computer system to draw conclusions from the use of a word or combination of words,
meaning must be identified with a finite collection of logical predicates (its
truth conditions) or procedures to be applied. Complications arise even
in apparently simple cases.

In classical discussions of semantics, the word "bachelor" has been put
forth as a word that can be clearly defined in more elementary terms:
"adult human male who has never been married."[4] But when someone
refers to a person as a "bachelor" in an ordinary conversational situation,
much more (and less) is conveyed. "Bachelor" is inappropriate if used in
describing the Pope or a member of a monogamous homosexual couple,
and might well be used in describing an independent career woman. The
problem is not that the definition of bachelor is complex and involves more
terms than accounted for in the classical definition. There is no coherent
'checklist' of any length such that objects meeting all of its conditions will
consistently be called "bachelors" and those failing one or more of them
will not.[5] The question "Is X a bachelor?" cannot be answered without
considering the potential answers to "Why do you want to know?" This
is what Gadamer means by "A question is behind each statement that
first gives it its meaning." It is possible to create artificial 'stipulative
definitions,' as in a mathematics text or in establishing the use of terms in

---

[4]This is, of course, only one of its definitions. Others, as pointed out in Katz and
Fodor's account of semantics ("The structure of a semantic theory," 1964), relate to
fur seals and chivalry.

[5]For a discussion of examples like this, see Fillmore, "An alternative to checklist
theories of meaning" (1975) and Winograd, "Toward a procedural understanding of
semantics" (1976).

legal documents, but these do not account for the normal use of language.

When we leave philosophical examples and look at the words appearing in everyday language, the problem becomes even more obvious. Each of the nouns in the sentence "The regime's corruption provoked a crisis of confidence in government" raises a significant problem for definition. It is clear that purpose and context play a major role in determining what will be called a "crisis," "corruption," or a "regime."

Other problems arise in trying to deal with words such as "the" and "and," which seem the closest to logical operators. In SHRDLU, as described above, the program for determining the referent of a definite noun phrase such as "the block" made use of a list of previously mentioned objects. The most recently mentioned thing fitting the description was assumed to be the referent. But this is only a rough approximation. Sometimes it gives a wrong answer, and other times it gives no clue at all. Consider the text: "Tommy had just been given a new set of blocks. He was opening the box when he saw Jimmy coming in."

> There is no mention of what is in the box—no clue as to what box it is at all. But a person reading the text makes the immediate assumption that it is the box which contains the set of blocks. We can do this because we know that new items often come in boxes, and that opening the box is a usual thing to do. Most important, we assume that we are receiving a connected message. There is no reason why the box has to be connected with the blocks, but if it weren't, it couldn't be mentioned without further introduction. — Winograd, "When will computers understand people?" (1974), p. 75.

The problem, then, is to account for how the background of knowledge and expectations leads to interpretation. In building artificial intelligence systems, this has led to the addition of 'internal' aspects to the representation. In addition to reasoning about the subject matter, the program attempts to model those aspects of the speaker's and hearer's internal thought processes that are relevant to interpretation. There has been a good deal of work along these lines[6] which rests on an extended version of the basic model and a corresponding extension of the assumptions given above:

1. There is a systematic way of correlating sentences in natural language with structures in the representation system.

---

[6]See, for example, Schank and Abelson, *Scripts Plans Goals and Understanding* (1977); Hobbs, "Coherence and coreference" (1979); Grosz, "Utterance and objective: Issues in natural language communication" (1980).

2. The correlation can be analyzed in terms of:

   (a) Fixed basic meanings of the smallest elements (words or morphemes).

   (b) Rules for the composition of these into the meanings of phrases and sentences, where these rules can take into account specific properties of the current state of speaker and hearer (including memory of the preceding text).

3. There is a fixed set of relevant properties that constitute the psychological state of a language user, and there is a well-defined set of rules that describe how this state is modified by any utterance.

The extension allows considerations such as recency, focus, and hearer's knowledge to contribute to the analysis of the meaning of an utterance. The third assumption is necessary or the second becomes vacuous. If we cannot specify the relevant properties and the laws that govern them, then we cannot have a rigorous account of meaning.

Philosophers have generally avoided making this kind of extension because of the difficulty of producing a clear account of psychological state as it relates to language.[7] Workers in artificial intelligence, on the other hand, adopt a pragmatic approach with casual introspection as a guide to devising models that seem potentially useful. Objects and properties get added to the representation of the state of the speaker/hearer because the programmer feels they will be relevant. They are kept because with them the system is perceived as in some way performing better than it did without them.

There have been many clever ideas for what should be included in the model of the speaker/hearer and how some of it might be organized, but the overall feeling is of undirected and untested speculation. Experimental psychology provides some suggestive concepts, but little else of direct use. A language comprehension system depends on models of memory, attention, and inference, all dealing with meaningful material, not the well-controlled stimuli of the typical laboratory experiment. Research in cognitive psychology has focussed on tasks that do not generalize to these more complex activities. In fact, much current psychological investigation of how people deal with meaningful material has been guided by research on artificial intelligence rather than the other way around.

---

[7] A partial exception is Barwise and Perry, (*Situations and Attitudes*, 1983), who attempt to situate these complexities in the tradition of analytic philosophy of language. Winograd, in "Moving the semantic fulcrum" (1985), discusses the relevance of their work for artificial intelligence.

9.3 Understanding as pattern recognition

The artificial intelligence literature of the 1970s heralded a move away from the traditional problem-solving orientation towards a new one centered around 'frames' or 'expectations.' Programs based on 'beta structures' (Moore and Newell, 1973), 'frames' (Minsky, 1975), 'scripts' (Schank and Abelson, 1977), 'schemas' (Bobrow and Norman, 1975), and 'prototypes' and 'perspectives' (Bobrow and Winograd, 1977) all deal with how a previously existing structure guides the interpretation of new inputs. The emphasis is on *recognition* rather than *problem solving*. It has been claimed that these systems avoid the limitations of earlier approaches to representation and that they support 'non-logical' kinds of reasoning that more closely approximate human intelligence. We will examine these claims in light of our discussion of background.

The overall idea is summarized by Minsky:

> Here is the essence of the theory: When one encounters a new situation (or makes a substantial change in one's view of the present problem) one selects from memory a substantial structure called a frame. This is a remembered framework to be adapted to fit reality by changing details as necessary.... Once a frame is proposed to represent a situation, a matching process tries to assign values to the terminals [the detailed features] of each frame, consistent with the markers at each place.... Most of the phenomenological power of the theory hinges on the inclusion of expectations and other kinds of presumptions. A frame's terminals are normally already filled with default assignments. Thus, a frame may contain a great many details whose supposition is not specifically warranted by the situation. These have many uses in representing general information, most-likely cases, techniques for 'bypassing logic' and ways to make useful generalizations. — Minsky, "A framework for representing knowledge" (1975), pp. 212-213.

Minsky's standard example is a frame for the visual appearance of a room. Once we have decided (perhaps on the basis of seeing a doorway) that we are looking at a room, our interpretation of the rest of the scene is biased by assumptions that certain other elements (such as windows) are present. Similar assumptions also apply to the understanding of a sentence, in which previous expectations are matched against the contents. In applying the frame idea to the meaning of words in a natural language, we associate a frame-like 'prototype' with each word. This prototype, like a definition, includes a description of the objects to which the word applies. Unlike a definition, however, this further description is not taken to be sufficient or necessary for determining the applicability of the word. It can include things that are typical (but not always the case) or that are relevant only in some contexts. In deciding whether a word applies to a representation of an object, the reasoning system compares these further descriptions to what is known about the object. In doing so it can preferentially deal with only some of the description, choosing what to do on the basis of context.

It would seem that a process of this type has the potential to treat word meanings in the open-ended way discussed for the "bachelor" example above. Although the "bachelor" prototype includes further descriptions (typical life style, age, etc.), the process of checking is context-dependent. One can devise strategies for deciding which of these to examine, depending on some characterization of context and current purposes.

In addition to using expectations about typical properties, frame systems have also been portrayed as a way to reason and understand by analogy.

> One thing that people remember is a particular experience, often in some detail. So, we postulate a level of memory that contains specific remembrances of particular situations.... Understanding is finding the closest higher-level structure available to explain an input and creating a new memory node for that input that is in terms of the old node's closely related higher-level structure. Understanding is a process that has its basis in memory, particularly memory for closely related experiences accessible through reminding and expressible through analogy. — Schank, "Language and memory" (1981), pp. 121, 129.

In a way, frame-based computational systems approach meaning from a hermeneutic direction. They concentrate not on the question "How does the program come to accurately reflect the situation?" but rather "How does the system's preknowledge (collection of frames) affect its interpretation of the situation?" The meaning of a sentence or scene lies in the interaction between its structure and the pre-existing structures in the machine.

The widespread enthusiasm about frames was a response to a shared but unarticulated awareness of the inadequacies of the problem-solving approach. But the solution did not solve the problems. Let us once again consider the task of a programmer trying to create an intelligent program, this time using frames. First there is the characterization of the task environment. This is essentially the same. It is still necessary to distinguish the relevant objects and properties before doing any representation.

The difference comes in the second step—in designing the formal system used to represent the situation. In more traditional programs, whether or not they explicitly use formal logic, there is an assumption that formulas represent propositions of the kind traditionally assigned truth values, such as "Every dog is an animal." A major goal of frame formalisms was to represent 'defaults': the ways things are typically, but not always. For example we might want to include the fact "Dogs bark" without precluding the possibility of a mute dog.

The frame intuition can be implemented only in a system that does informal reasoning—one that comes to conclusions based on partial evidence, makes assumptions about what is relevant and what is to be expected in typical cases, and leaves open the possibility of mistake and contradiction. It can be 'non-monotonic'—it can draw some conclusion, then reverse it on the basis of further information.[8]

The problem, of course, is to know when something is to be treated as 'typical' and when the various parts of the frame are to be taken as relevant. Here, if we look at the literature on frame systems, we find a mixture of hand waving and silence. Simple rules don't work. If, for example, defaults are used precisely when there is no explicit (previously derived) information to the contrary, then we will assume that one holds even when a straightforward simple deduction might contradict it. If analogies are treated too simply, we attempt to carry over the detailed properties of one object to another for which they are not appropriate.

It should be clear that the answer cannot lie in extending the details of the rules within the subject domain. If the default that rooms have windows is to be applied precisely in the cases of "those rooms that... and not those that..." then it is no longer a default. We have simply refined our description of the world to distinguish among more properties that rooms can have.

Another approach has been to postulate 'resource-limited processing' as a basis for reasoning.[9] In any act of interpretation or reasoning, a system (biological or computer) has a finite quantity of processing resources to expend. The nature of these resources will be affected by the details of the processor, its environment, and its previous history. The outcome of the process is determined by the interaction between the structure of the task and the allocation of processing. The ability to deal with partial or imprecise information comes from the ability to do a finite amount of processing, then jump to a conclusion on the basis of what has happened so far, even though that conclusion may not be deducible or even true.

---

[8] For a variety of approaches to non-monotonic reasoning, see the papers in Bobrow (ed.), "Special issue on non-monotonic logic" (1980).

[9] For a general discussion of resource-limited processing as applied to experimental psychology, see Norman and Bobrow, "On data-limited and resource-limited processes" (1975).

This is what Minsky refers to when he talks of the need to "bypass logic."

From one point of view, a resource-limited system is a purely logical formal system—it operates with precise rules on well-defined structures, as does any computer program. From another viewpoint the system is carrying out informal reasoning. The key to this paradox lies in the use of formal rules that are relative to the structure of the computer system that embodies the formalism.[10] In reasoning about some task environment, a frame-based system can come to conclusions on the basis not only of statements about the world, but also on the basis of the form of the representation and the processes that manipulate it (for example, concluding something is false because it is represented as typically false, and with some bounded amount of deduction in this case it cannot be proved true).

Once again, the intuition is related to the work we have been presenting. Maturana's account of structure-determined systems deals directly with how the system's structure (rather than an externally observed structure of the environment) determines its space of operation. However, there is a significant difference in that the frame approach assumes a mechanism operating on representations, albeit in a resource-limited way.

Although the general idea of frames with resource-limited reasoning has some plausibility, it has not produced computer systems with any degree of generality. The problem lies in accounting for how the detailed structure of the system leads to the desired results. Only very simplistic examples have been given of what this structure might look like, and those examples cannot be extended in any obvious way. Programs actually written using frame systems tend to fall into two classes. Either the structures are written with a few specific examples in mind and work well only for those examples and minor variations on them,[11] or they do not make any essential use of the frame ideas (adopting only a frame-like notation) and are equivalent to more traditional programs.[12]

Furthermore, even if a system containing frames with an appropriate structure could be constructed, it still does not escape the problems of blindness described in Chapter 8. The programmer is responsible for a characterization of the objects and properties to be dealt with using frames, to exactly the same degree as the programmer of any representation system. The program begins with a characterization of the possible objects and properties. Detailed consideration of its internal structure (both of representations and of processes on them) cannot move beyond

---

[10]Hofstadter, in *Gödel, Escher, Bach* (1979) elaborates this point clearly and at great length.

[11]See, for example, the programs described in Schank, "Language and memory" (1981).

[12]This was the experience with KRL, as described in Bobrow et al., "Experience with KRL-0" (1977).

this initial articulation. No amount of non-monotonic resource-limited processing in this domain can lead to giving the program a background in the sense of pre-understanding emphasized by Heidegger or the structural coupling described by Maturana.

9.4 What does it mean to understand?

In light of this critique, we may be puzzled when *Newsweek* reports that "Computers can...draw analogies among Shakespearean plays and understand tales involving friendship and adultery"[13] and Schank and Riesbeck state that their program SAM "was a major advance...because its use of scripts allowed it to understand real stories."[14] Are these claims true or false?

To answer this last question in its own terms would violate our theory of language. If objective truth conditions cannot be defined for "water," how could they possibly be found for "understand"? We need instead to analyze the web of commitments into which we have entered when we seriously utter a sentence of the form "X understands Y." We will begin by illustrating some simple 'language understanding' programs as a basis for comparison.

Program 1 prints out the time of day whenever the precise sequence "What time is it?" is typed in. Any other sequence is simply ignored. Such a program might well operate to the satisfaction of those who use it, and they might want to claim that it "understands the question," since it responds appropriately.

Program 2 accepts sequences of the form "What ... is it?" where the gap is filled by "time," "day," "month," or "year." It types out the appropriate answer to each of these and ignores any sequence not matching this pattern.

Program 3 has a collection of patterns that are matched against the input. For each of these there is a corresponding form to be printed out, where that printout may include fragments of the pattern that was entered. The program finds a pattern that matches the input and prints out the associated response. For example if it is provided with the pattern "My name is ..." and corresponding response "Hello, ..., how are you today?" it would respond to the input "My name is Joseph" with "Hello, Joseph, how are you today?"

---

[13]Begley et al., "How smart can computers get?" (1980), p. 52.

[14]*Inside Computer Understanding* (1981), p. 6.

Those familiar with artificial intelligence will recognize program 3 as ELIZA.[15] This program was run (under the name DOCTOR) with a collection of patterns that simulated a non-directive psychiatrist interviewing a patient. For example, it responded to "I am ..." with "How long have you been ... ?" Given "I hope ..." it responded "What would it mean to you if ... ?" and given "... everybody ..." it responded "Are you thinking of somebody in particular?"

The behavior of the DOCTOR program was strikingly human-like. Weizenbaum reported:

> I was startled to see how quickly and how very deeply people conversing with DOCTOR became emotionally involved with the computer and how unequivocally they anthropomorphized it.... Another widespread, and to me surprising, reaction to the ELIZA program was the spread of a belief that it demonstrated a general solution to the problem of computer understanding of natural language. — Weizenbaum, *Computer Power and Human Reason* (1976), p. 6.

Program 4 has a collection of 'scripts,' each corresponding to a particular kind of event sequence. For example, it might have a script for what happens when a person goes to a restaurant: "The person enters, is seated by a host, is brought a menu by a waiter, orders some food, is brought the food by the waiter, eats the food, is brought a check by the waiter, pays the check, and leaves." When an input is entered that matches the 'title' of the script (i.e., it mentions going to a restaurant), the program then compares each subsequent input with one of the event patterns in the script and fills in values based on the input (as ELIZA filled in the "..." in the examples above). If the input does not match the next event in line, it skips over that event and compares it to the next. Once the input is complete, the program can use the values filled in from the inputs to answer simple questions. For example, given the sequence of inputs "John went to a restaurant. John ate a hamburger," it can use the script to answer the question "What did John order?" with "a hamburger."

Again, this is a description (slightly simplified but not in any essential way) of an existing program—the SAM program that Schank and Riesbeck described as "understanding real stories." It has served as a model for a series of more elaborate programs done by Schank and his group, as described in Schank and Riesbeck, *Inside Computer Understanding* (1981).

---

[15]Weizenbaum, "ELIZA" (1966).

With these examples in mind, let us return to the question of what it would mean for a computer to understand language. We might say that the computer understands when it responds appropriately. The obvious problem lies in determining what constitutes an appropriate response. In one sense, the simple clock program always responds appropriately. Asked "What time is it?" it types out the time. But of course we could equally well have designed it to respond with the time when we type in "Why is the sky blue?" or simply "?" The appropriateness of the response is relative to a background of other things that might be said. In the case of the timekeeper (or the more elaborate program 2 that allows some variability in the patterns) this range is too limited to warrant being called understanding.

But as we move up in complexity to ELIZA and SAM, the essential issue doesn't change. The range of patterns grows larger and, as Weizenbaum reports, it may be difficult for a person to recognize the program's limitations. Nonetheless, the program responds on the basis of a fixed set of patterns provided by a programmer who anticipated certain inputs. This anticipation may be clever (as in the DOCTOR's response to sentences mentioning "everybody"), but it still represents a permanent structure of blindness. This limitation is not one of insufficient deductive power. It applies equally to programs like SHRDLU that include routines for reasoning with representations, and holds as well for systems with 'frame-like' reasoning. It lies in the nature of the process by which representations are fixed in a computer program.

It is important to recognize that this limitation is not dependent on the apparent breadth of subject. SHRDLU operates in a microworld in which the set of objects, properties, and relations are fixed and limited in an obvious way. The DOCTOR apparently deals with all aspects of human life, but it is really working with an even more limited set of objects and properties, as specified in its patterns. Given the sentence "I am swallowing poison," it will respond "How long have you been swallowing poison?" rather than responding as a person would to implications that were not anticipated in creating the pattern.

The claim that computers "understand tales involving friendship and adultery" was based on a program called BORIS,[16] a more elaborate version of SAM. Instead of dealing with "John went to a restaurant. He ate a hamburger," BORIS works on stories containing sentences like "When Paul walked into the bedroom and found Sarah with another man, he nearly had a heart attack. Then he realized what a blessing it was." It responds to questions like "What happened to Paul at home?" and "How

---

[16]Lehnert et al., "BORIS: An experiment in in-depth understanding of narratives" (1983).

did Paul feel?" with "Paul caught Sarah committing adultery" and "Paul was surprised."

If we examine the workings of BORIS we find a menagerie of script-like representations (called MOPS, TOPS, TAUS, and META-MOPS) that were used in preparing the system for the one specific story it could answer questions about. For example, TAU-RED-HANDED is activated "when a goal to violate a norm, which requires secrecy for its success, fails during plan execution due to a witnessing." It characterizes the feeling of the witness as "surprised." In order to apply this to the specific story, there are MOPS such as M-SEX (which is applied whenever two people are in a bedroom together) and M-ADULTERY (which includes the structure needed to match the requirements of TAU-RED-HANDED). The apparent human breadth of the program is like that of ELIZA. A rule that "If two people are in a bedroom together, infer they are having sex" is as much a micro-world inference as "If one block is directly above another, infer that the the lower one supports the upper." The illusions described by Weizenbaum are fueled by subject matter that makes it appear that complex and subtle understanding is taking place.

In a similar vein, the program that can "draw analogies among Shakespearean plays" operates in a micro-world that the programmer fashioned after his reading of Shakespeare.[17] The actual input is not a Shakespeare play, or even a formal representation of the lines spoken by the characters, but a structure containing a few objects and relations based on the plot. The complete representation of *Macbeth* used for drawing analogies consisted of the following:

> {Macbeth is a noble} before {Macbeth is a king}.
> Macbeth marry Lady-Macbeth.
> Lady-Macbeth is a woman—has-property greedy ambitious.
> Duncan is a king.
> Macduff is a noble—has-property loyal angry.
> Weird-sisters is a hag group—has-property old ugly weird—
>   number 3.
> Weird-sisters predict {Macbeth murder Duncan}.
> Macbeth desire {Macbeth kind-of king}
>   [cause {Macbeth murder Duncan}].
> Lady-Macbeth persuade {Macbeth murder Duncan}.
> Macbeth murder Duncan {coagent Lady-Macbeth—
>   instrument knife}.
> Lady-Macbeth kill Lady-Macbeth.
> Macbeth murder Duncan [cause{Macduff kill Macbeth}].

---

[17]Winston, "Learning and reasoning by analogy" (1980).

The program includes simple rules like "whenever a person persuades another to do an action, the action is caused by the persuasion and the persuaded person has 'control' of the action." As with all of the examples so far, the program's claim to understanding is based on the fact that the linguistic and experiential domains the programmer is trying to represent are complex and call for a broad range of human understanding. As with the other examples, however, the program actually operates within a narrowed micro-world that reflects the blindness of that representation.

But, one might argue, aren't people subject to this blindness too? If we don't want to describe these programs as 'understanding language,' how can we coherently ascribe understanding to anyone? To answer this we must return to the theory of language presented in Chapter 5. We argued there that the essence of language as a human activity lies not in its ability to reflect the world, but in its characteristic of creating commitment. When we say that a person understands something, we imply that he or she has entered into the commitment implied by that understanding. But how can a computer enter into a commitment?

As we pointed out in Chapter 8, the use of mental terms like "understand" presupposes an orientation towards an autonomous agent. In spite of this, it is often convenient to use mental terms for animals and machines. It seems natural to say "This program only understands commands asking for the time and date" and to find this way of talking effective in explaining behavior. In this case, "understand a command" means to perform those operations that someone intends to invoke in giving the command. But the computer is not committed to behaving in this way—it is committed to nothing. I do not attribute to it the kind of responsibility that I would to a person who obeyed (or failed to obey) the same words.

Of course there is a commitment, but it is that of the programmer, not the program. If I write something and mail it to you, you are not tempted to see the paper as exhibiting language behavior. It is a medium through which you and I interact. If I write a complex computer program that responds to things you type, the situation is still the same—the program is still a medium through which my commitments to you are conveyed. This intermediation is not trivial, and in Chapter 12 we will describe the roles that computers can play as an 'active structured communication medium.' Nonetheless, it must be stressed that we are engaging in a particularly dangerous form of blindness if we see the computer—rather than the people who program it—as doing the understanding.

This applies equally to systems like TEIRESIAS[18] that can respond to queries about the details of the representation itself and the way it has been used in a particular calculation. The 'meta-knowledge' programmed

---

[18]Davis, "Interactive transfer of expertise" (1979).

into such a system is a representation of exactly the kind we have been talking about throughout this book. It may play a useful role in the operation of the program, but it reflects a pre-determined choice of objects, properties, and relations and is limited in its description of the program in the same way the program is limited in its description of a domain. Hofstadter argues in *Gödel, Escher, Bach* (1979) that these limitations might not apply to a system that allows multiple levels of such knowledge, including 'strange loops' in which a level of description applies to itself. However, he admits that this is an unsupported intuition, and is not able to offer explanations of just why we should expect such systems to be really different.

As we have pointed out in earlier chapters, a person is not permanently trapped in the same kind of blindness. We have the potential to respond to breakdown with a shift of domains in which we enter into new commitments. Understanding is not a fixed relationship between a representation and the things represented, but is a commitment to carry out a dialog within the full horizons of both speaker and hearer in a way that permits new distinctions to emerge.

What does all this mean about practical applications of language processing on computers? Our critique is not a condemnation of the technical work that has been done or even of the specific techniques (representations, deductive logic, frames, meta-description, etc.) that have been developed. It challenges the common understanding of how these techniques are related to the human use of language. Chapter 10 describes some practical applications of computer programs in which linguistic structures (e.g., English words and syntax) provide a useful medium for building or accessing formal representations. The deductive techniques developed in artificial intelligence (including the frame-like reasoning discussed in this chapter) may serve well in producing useful responses by such programs.

What is important is that people using the system recognize (as those duped by ELIZA did not) two critical things. First, they are using the structures of their natural language to interact with a system that does not understand the language but is able to manipulate some of those structures. Second, the responses reflect a particular representation that was created by some person or group of people, and embodies a blindness of which even the builders cannot be fully aware.

Chapter 10

Current directions in artificial intelligence

There is an apparent contradiction between our critical view of the potential for artificial intelligence and the current mood of optimistic expansion that dominates research and development in the area. During the past few years, AI has moved from being a laboratory curiosity to seeking a major role in technology policy and investment. In his 1981 presidential address to the American Association for Artificial Intelligence, Feigenbaum described the first surge of enthusiasm:

> No one who attended the First National AAAI conference last August at Stanford could fail to be impressed by the size and quality of the scientific meeting and the power of the ideas presented.... Eleven hundred scientists, engineers, R&D managers, students, venture capitalists and journalists gathered.... Mingled with the usual scientific papers were discussions of impending industrial applications and the motives of the companies (mighty and midget) who are now entering the field because of its potential for application. — Feigenbaum, "AAAI President's message" (1980/81), p. 1.

Even within the traditionally conservative business community there has been a campaign to foster optimism and to promote financial interest in artificial intelligence ventures:

> The world stands on the threshold of a second computer age. New technology now moving out of the laboratory is starting to change the computer from a fantastically fast calculating machine to a device that mimics human thought processes—giving

machines the capability to reason, make judgments, and even learn.... Experts are convinced that it is now only a matter of time before these 'thinking' computers open up awesome new applications in offices, factories, and homes. — *Business Week,* "Artificial Intelligence: The second computer age begins" (1982), p. 66.

Computers... emerged decades ago to mechanize the process of converting raw data into information that humans could comprehend and use in decision-making. Now we are entering the era in which they will convert information into knowledge— showing us how to design computers, find valuable ore deposits, and otherwise accomplish our purposes. Perhaps a day will come when they will begin converting knowledge to wisdom— advising us as to what purposes are truly worth accomplishing. — Alexander, "Computers on the road to self-improvement" (1982), p. 160.

These statements might well be dismissed as pure fantasy. Advice on 'what purposes are truly worth accomplishing' is so obviously outside the scope of computation that it indicates a deep misunderstanding of what computers do. However, this kind of discussion has a significant effect on our shared background of understanding about computers, and we need to be able to distinguish fantasy from genuine potential for development. This chapter examines more closely the current state of research in artificial intelligence and the burgeoning interest in commercial applications.

10.1   The forking of the paths

Until the mid-1970s artificial intelligence researchers generally believed they could work simultaneously towards two goals: extending the capabilities of computers, and moving towards an understanding of human intelligence. They might emphasize one aspect or the other, choosing to call their work 'artificial intelligence' or 'cognitive simulation,' but that was a short-term strategic decision, aimed towards an ultimate synthesis.

In the last few years, this view has been questioned. There is a tacit acceptance of the point we have made in this book—that the techniques of current AI are not adequate for an understanding of human thought and language. As a result, there is a clear split between the 'knowledge engineers,' who apply the well-developed technologies of AI to practical problems, and the 'mind-modelers,' who speculate about the more complex structures that might underlie human thought.

Commercial interest lies in the first direction—in finding profitable applications of a rather limited set of techniques. The greatest interest is in 'expert systems'—programs for problem solving in some scientific or technical domain. We will discuss these more fully in the following section. First we will look at the less extensive current developments in robotics and natural language processing and at the work aimed more in the direction of cognitive modelling.

Robotics

In the early years of artificial intelligence, work on robotics emphasized the quest for general principles of intelligence underlying human perception and action. Abstract work on symbolic problem solving was motivated by plans for a robot operating with a 'hand' or maneuvering its way around an environment. Current work in robotics applies some techniques developed in this earlier work, but is better understood as extending a process of automation that began decades ago.

Computers already play a major role in the physical work of industry, for example in controlling the complex processes of oil refineries and in guiding numerically controlled milling machines. As computer hardware becomes cheaper, it becomes practical to automate more activities:

> Several of the largest U.S. corporations are making major commitments to the use of industrial robots.... Three top computer companies... are seriously considering jumping into the robot market.... New technology is making it possible to replace increasingly skilled workers. The latest computer-controlled robots are considerably more versatile than their simple-minded predecessors of just two years ago. And a new generation of robots that 'see' and 'feel' and even 'think' is emerging from the laboratories. — *Business Week*, "Robots join the labor force" (1980), p. 62.

Once again we need to be cautious about words like 'think' (even when set off in quotation marks). Nevertheless it is quite likely that automation will continue to develop, including general-purpose programmable manipulators and visual-manual coordination. It is not within the scope of this book to analyze the economic potential for such systems or to discuss the social effects of their widespread use. However, it is important to separate out the real potential for such devices from the implications that come from calling them applications of artificial 'intelligence,' and even from the use of the word 'robot.'

This book has not focussed on aspects of intelligence directly concerned with perception and action in a physical world. As we discussed in Chapter

8, this is not because the issues are different, but because the central focus of the argument is clearer in 'disembodied' areas. The limitations of representation and programming based on a formal characterization of properties and actions are just as strong (if not stronger) in dealing with physical robots. Perception is much more than the encoding of an external world into a representation, and action is more than the execution of 'motor routines.' Nevertheless, robotic devices that operate in artificially limited domains may be quite useful, in spite of (or at times because of) not reflecting the nature of human perception and action.

Natural language interaction

Another area of active commercial development is the creation of 'natural language front ends.' As in other areas, the advertising often far outstrips the content of the research. One company, for example, advertises "programs that understand you so that you don't have to understand them."[1] Their brochure goes on to say:

> Cognitive Systems, Inc. creates and markets computer software that is revolutionizing data processing, resulting in immense benefits in terms of employee productivity and information accessibility. Our programs understand English—not an English-like programming language but *everyday conversational English* [emphasis in the original] (or French or German or any language you want).... Cognitive Systems natural language programs are unique in that they are intelligent.... We give our computer programs the same kind of knowledge that people use, so our programs understand a sentence just the way a person does, and respond in conversational English.

Even those who believe in the success of artificial intelligence view such claims as a gross exaggeration of the capabilities of any existing system. They are all the more notable since the company is directed by one of the leading figures in artificial intelligence research, who is also chairman of the computer science department at a major university.[2]

---

[1]Advertising brochure for Cognitive Systems, Inc., distributed at the AAAI National Conference, August 1982.

[2]From the brochure: "Cognitive Systems, Inc. is an outgrowth of research at the Artificial Intelligence (AI) Lab of the Computer Science Department at Yale University. The Yale AI Lab is one of the foremost research centers in the country in the field of natural language processing. Cognitive Systems was founded by Professor Roger Schank, Chairman of the Computer Science Department and Director of Research at the AI Lab at Yale."

More responsible proponents of natural language interaction acknowledge that programs cannot understand language in a significant sense, and argue that many practical applications may not demand real understanding. In some applications the structures of natural language provide a useful way to interact with a computer system carrying out a limited task. The interaction can be for control (as in giving instructions to a manipulator) or for information retrieval (as in getting statistics from a data base). A number of companies and research laboratories are designing natural language 'front ends' to data base systems, for both mainframes and personal computers. Such a program transforms input sentences into well-formed queries that the data base system can process. The limitation of scope and domain comes naturally from the limitations of the data base itself.

The practicality of limited natural language systems is still an open question. Since the nature of the queries is limited by the formal structure of the data base, it may well be more efficient for a person to learn a specialized formal language designed for that purpose, rather than learning through experience just which English sentences will and will not be handled. When interacting in natural language it is easy to fall into assuming that the range of sentences that can be appropriately processed will approximate what would be understood by a human being with a similar collection of data. Since this is not true, the user ends up adapting to a collection of idioms—fixed patterns that experience has shown will work. Once the advantage of flexibility has been removed, it is not clear that the additional costs of natural language (verbosity, redundancy, ambiguity, etc.) are worth paying in place of a more streamlined formal system. On the other hand, there are cases in which the appearance of natural language can make a computer system seem less formidable, encouraging use by people who would resist a more visibly formal approach.

Some of the specific technologies developed in conjunction with artificial intelligence language research will lead to practical system developments. For example, speech recognition systems provide a form of communication that is more ready-to-hand than pressing keys on a keyboard. Customers will be disappointed if they expect the computer to understand spoken language as a person does. But it can identify sequences of sounds and trigger actions on the basis of them, within a limited domain. Machines can currently recognize a vocabulary of a few hundred items (words or short phrases). They will soon be extended to larger vocabularies and will be able to analyze more elaborate artificial syntactic structures that parallel some of the structures of natural language. The fact that computers cannot understand human language does not preclude the utility of interacting with them by voice. In fact, our theoretical understanding of tools leads us to believe that it will have many advantages.

Cognitive modelling

The widely publicized application developments stand in contrast to research aimed at the theoretical issues underlying human cognition. As mentioned above, current work is less ambitious in scope than were the earlier attempts. At the Massachusetts Institute of Technology Artificial Intelligence Laboratory, for example, work on detailed visual processes in the retina has displaced earlier vision work that dealt with higher-level object perception and 'frames.'[3] This is not to say that at MIT (or elsewhere) there is no longer any research in the classical AI style of applying representational techniques to general human abilities. But such work is taking a back seat to more specific analysis of 'peripheral' capabilities, and among some workers is being displaced by highly speculative attempts to characterize higher-level mental architecture.

This last direction is interesting because it has led to a rekindling of interest in issues that were prominent in earlier cybernetic research but had been previously rejected in AI. For example, there is new interest in phenomena of learning, and in the metaphorical use of 'stored experience' as a basis for understanding. Both of these were de-emphasized in the AI of the '60s and early '70s, since they were not amenable to the formal analysis and programming techniques that were then being developed. Their return to favor goes along with the acceptance that the available techniques are too limited to form the basis for a broad theory. The alternative has been the development of sketchy and loosely formulated descriptions of mental structures in 'connectionist' approaches, such as the 'society of minds' (Minsky, "The society theory of thinking," 1979), 'K-lines,' (Minsky, "K-Lines: A theory of memory," 1981), and 'Memory Organizing Packets' (Schank, "Language and memory," 1981). The desire for computational rigor has been abandoned in an attempt to touch on the more subtle aspects of thought and language.

As with the research on frames described in Chapter 9, the problem with these efforts lies in the huge gap between the subtlety of the intuitions that motivate them and the paucity of computational mechanisms that can produce behavior compatible with those intuitions. At times, justification for the theory seems to be little more than the hope that if the computational system is complex enough and its behavior sufficiently unpredictable, something intelligent will emerge.

Other researchers are looking towards the design of systems that 'learn' through training sequences, rather than being programmed. Programs like Lenat's EURISKO ("Computer software for intelligent systems," 1984) are started with a basic set of objects and properties, and with heuristics for

---

[3]For an overview of the newer approaches to vision, see Marr, *Vision* (1982).

combining them in various ways and testing the effectiveness of those combinations. As we discussed in the section on learning in Chapter 8, this does not enable them to move beyond the limitations of their initial domain. Similarly, detailed theories may be developed that in some way model the functioning of nervous systems and the modification of their structure over time. There is much to be discovered about how our nervous systems really work, but AI theories and neurophysiological theories are in different domains. Detailed theories of neurological mechanisms will not be the basis for answering the general questions about intelligence and understanding that have been raised in this book any more than detailed theories of transistor electronics would aid in understanding the complexities of computer software.

10.2 Expert systems

The area of artificial intelligence arousing the greatest commercial interest is the creation of systems that perform some detailed technical task, such as analyzing chemical spectrograms (Lindsay et al., *DENDRAL*, 1980), identifying a particular kind of bacterial infection (Shortliffe, *Computer Based Medical Consultations: MYCIN*, 1976), or checking a proposed configuration of computer equipment (McDermott, "R1: A rule-based configurer of computer systems," 1982).

These programs are based on rather straightforward techniques that were developed in the early work in artificial intelligence. They do not try to deal with the difficult questions of relevance, context, and background raised in earlier chapters of this book. They are built on the assumption that the programmer can determine a small clear classification of relevant objects and properties together with a set of rules relating them. They are applicable only to carefully limited domains. Buchanan, ("New research on expert systems," 1982, p. 283) lists some characteristics of problems that are suitable, including: "Narrow domain of expertise; limited language for expressing facts and relations; limiting assumptions about problem and solution methods; little knowledge of own scope and limitations." He is careful to label these limitations as being relative to the current 'state of the art,' but his observations are really more general. As we discussed at length in Chapter 8, these are exactly the characteristics that make it possible to create a program to do 'problem solving' within a systematic domain, and there is no reason to believe that any future state of the art will transcend them.

There are many areas of technology that are served by carrying out complex computations, of which AI techniques are one specialized kind. We expect such uses to continue proliferating, as they have ever since the earliest computers were used for code breaking and ballistic calculations. To the extent that areas can be well-defined and the rules for them set down precisely, 'expert systems' can be created and will operate successfully. However, there are two important caveats.

First, there is a danger inherent in the label 'expert system.' When we talk of a human 'expert' we connote someone whose depth of understanding serves not only to solve specific well-formulated problems, but also to put them into a larger context. We distinguish between experts and 'idiot savants.' Calling a program an 'expert' is misleading in exactly the same way as calling it 'intelligent' or saying it 'understands.' The misrepresentation may be useful for those who are trying to get research funding or sell such programs, but it can lead to inappropriate expectations by those who attempt to use them. Dreyfus and Dreyfus (*Mind Over Machine*, 1985) describe four stages of progressively greater expertise, of which only the first, 'novice' stage, can be accounted for with the kind of rules that have been used by programs attempting to duplicate expert performance.

The second problem with creating 'expert systems' is the difficulty in understanding and conveying a sense of the limitations of a particular program and of the approach in general. A good example of the problem can be found in the application of computers to medicine. Nobody would question that there are relevant computations (such as the determination of electrolyte balances) that are too complex for practical hand calculations. There are other areas (such as the recognition of specific infections and the analysis of electrocardiograms) in which the domain can be circumscribed carefully enough so that programs can be effective even though there is no simple 'closed form' algorithm for getting the 'right answer.' But in the popular press (and much of the professional literature as well), computers are described as 'diagnosing diseases' and 'choosing treatments.'

An editorial in the prestigious *New England Journal of Medicine* evaluated the potential for computer diagnosis:

> The optimistic expectation of 20 years ago that computer technology would also come to play an important part in clinical decisions has not been realized, and there are few if any situations in which computers are being routinely used to assist in either medical diagnosis or the choice of therapy.... In the real world it is necessary that the doctor not only understand the statistical relations of signs and symptoms to the various possible diseases but also have the wisdom and common sense that derive from the understanding and experience of everyday human existence. It is this last requirement that represents the greatest weakness (and perhaps the ultimate limitation) of computer technology in dealing in any comprehensive fash-

ion with the problem of clinical diagnosis. — Barnett, "The computer and clinical judgment" (1982), pp. 493-494.

In order to produce a set of rules for a medical 'expert' system, it is first necessary to pre-select the relevant factors and thereby cut out the role of the background. But as we have been arguing throughout this book, this process by its very nature creates blindness. There is always a limit set by what has been made explicit, and always the potential of breakdowns that call for moving beyond this limit.

The problem is not just that the designers of such programs can get people to believe the computer does more than it actually does, but that the designers themselves are blind to the limitations. Much of the current enthusiasm for applied artificial intelligence comes from the belief that the rather limited domains of applicability of current programs are just initial steps towards programs that really can do diagnosis and select treatments. As the work develops, serious researchers will gain a better understanding of the problems they are attacking, and we will eventually see a separation between those who persist in looking for intelligence in their programs and those who build programs that successfully carry out computations within carefully delimited domains.

10.3   The fifth generation computer system

Until recently, artificial intelligence research was pursued almost exclusively in the United States and Britain, with a small scattering of work in Europe and elsewhere. Japanese scientists followed with interest, but produced little new research. They are now trying to change that with the widely publicized 'fifth generation' computer project, initiated in 1981.[4] Their intent is to produce computer systems for the 1990s, making use of the latest developments in artificial intelligence and extending them to new uses and capabilities. After a two-year study involving dozens

---

[4]The name 'fifth generation' is based on a frequently used classification of earlier computer technologies. The first generation, developed in the 1940s, used vacuum tubes as computing elements. The second generation, in the mid '50s, replaced these with transistors, greatly increasing reliability and reducing costs. The third generation, in the '60s and early '70s, used 'integrated circuits' which combined the equivalent of many transistors and connections on a single chip. The fourth generation, of the '70s and '80s, uses 'very large scale integration' (VLSI) in which tens of thousands of circuit elements occupy a single silicon chip, making possible the 'micro-computer' that has revolutionized the use of computers.

For a thorough and careful discussion of the fifth generation project and its political context, see Uttal, "Here comes Computer Inc." (1982). Feigenbaum and McCorduck's *The Fifth Generation* (1983) was an attempt to stir up enthusiasm for a similar program in the United States.

of researchers, the Japanese Ministry of International Trade and Industry (MITI) decided to sponsor an ambitious ten-year project at a newly formed research center in Tokyo, called the Institute for New Generation Computer Technology. It was anticipated that the overall ten-year project would involve an investment of at least $500 million, and perhaps several times that.[5]

The announcement of this commitment to push computer technology in a new direction came when the United States and Europe are in a period of crisis and self-doubt about productivity and the effective development of technology. Japan's success in world markets (especially in high-technology products) has been extolled, denounced, and scrutinized in agonizing detail. As might be expected, the fifth generation project has created a great deal of interest. There have been responses from several nations, eager not to be left behind. In Britain, a committee chaired by Lord Alvey (1982) successfully advocated a major new spending plan in computing research. On the continent, the Common Market (EEC) created a program called Esprit, to sponsor multinational research efforts within the Common Market. A French report (CNSRS, 1983) on the need for a "Programme de Development de l'Intelligence Artificielle" was summarized: "This report insists on prompt action: there is no further time to be lost." In the United States, the major response has been from the Defense Advanced Research Projects Agency (DARPA), which has long been the primary sponsor of artificial intelligence research. It initiated the Strategic Computing Initiative with the intent to invest $500 million over the next ten years to develop artificial intelligence technology oriented to specific military goals.[6]

The fifth generation project and its followers raise many important issues concerning the development of technology and the roles of government and industry in research. In this book, however, we will concentrate on the theoretical issues: What are these projects really trying to do, and what would it mean to achieve it?

The goals are anything but modest. In his introduction to the study initiating the fifth generation project, the project leader stated:

> Fifth generation computers are expected to function extremely effectively in all fields of society.... Totally new applied fields will be developed, social productivity will be increased, and distortions in values will be eliminated.... Everyone will be able to converse with computers even without a professional

---

[5]By late 1984, the projection had been reduced by about half, due to serious deficits and budget cuts by the Japanese government.

[6]For an analysis and critique of this program see Davis, "Assessing the Strategic Computing Initiative" (1985).

knowledge of them, even if everyday natural language is used, the computers will be able to understand our thoughts and give us suitable answers.... By promoting the study of artificial intelligence and realizing intelligent robots, a better understanding of the mechanisms of life will become possible. The approaching realization of automatic interpretation and translation will serve to help people of different tongues understand each other, to reduce troubles due to misunderstanding and ignorance, and to lead to further growth based on mutual understanding of cultures. With the construction of a knowledge base made possible, the knowledge which mankind has accumulated can be stored and effectively utilized, so that the development of culture as a whole can be rapidly promoted. — Moto-oka, "Keynote speech: Challenge for knowledge information processing systems" (1982), pp. 23-24.

The first page of the study lists four major social areas in which fifth generation computers will "play active roles in the resolving of anticipated social bottlenecks":

1. Increasing productivity in low productivity areas such as agriculture, fishing, goods distribution, and public services.

2. Meeting international competition and contributing toward international cooperation through the development of information-intensive industries.

3. Assisting in saving energy and resources by improving efficiency of resource use and developing knowledge-intensive (rather than resource-intensive) industry.

4. Coping with an aging society through such advances as streamlined medical and related information systems, health management systems, and lifetime education systems.

All of this will take major advances in the technology, characterized in terms such as "increase the level of computer intelligence as well as their affinity for cooperation with man," "use their vast ability to store information to achieve new judgment facilities of their own," and "[increase] the intelligence level of computers... to the extent where they can comprehend the environment."

It should be obvious how our critique of artificial intelligence applies to this plan. It is naive to say that computers of any generation will be able to "understand our thoughts" or "comprehend the environment," and it

is unrealistic to expect that they will have a major positive impact on the
wide variety of problems identified by Moto-oka.

However, the more detailed plans appearing in the same study give
a somewhat different perspective. The project is not a monolithic push
towards a single goal, but an attempt to promote and coordinate research
on advanced computer technology in a quite general way. Although the
artificial intelligence aspect gets the most attention in public descriptions,
it is only one component of a full spectrum of computer science research.

To the extent that there is a common theme tying the project together,
we can summarize it as a loosely linked series of research commitments:

1. Computer technology can play a major role in solving social problems.

2. The major technical problem is to increase the effectiveness of human
   use of computers.

3. This will be achieved through the development of 'intelligent' systems along the lines of current expert systems and artificial intelligence research.

4. Expert systems will become much more advanced when built using
   specialized machines and programming languages especially suited
   to them.

5. These new machines will make use of parallel processing (the ability
   to carry on many computations simultaneously) much more than
   current computers.

6. The construction of such machines will require the development of
   advanced VLSI techniques.

Many of the steps in this chain can stand on their own. It is no novelty
to say that the human-computer interface is a prime area for research or
that new advances will come from parallel machine architectures. Many of
the specific research themes deal with one or another of the steps above,
and their success or failure will stand independently of the chain of reasoning. The project will produce useful results even if it does not increase
productivity in agriculture or significantly improve the quality of life for
the aged. Let us consider each of these steps more carefully.

1. **Can computer technology play a major role in solving social
   problems?** As with any technology, there are potential benefits and
   dangers. There is no question that computers will have major effects
   on society, as they already have. While this provides an important

motivation for technical development, we must not fall into the trap of assuming that the technology will fix the problems. In the case of computers there is a double temptation, since if the direct application of computer technology to the problems is not the answer, one might hope for 'intelligent' programs that can tell us what to do. As we emphasized in Chapter 8, this is an idle dream.

2. **Is the major technical problem to increase the effectiveness with which people use computers?** Here, we are quite in agreement with the basic idea, but not with its expression. Indeed, the way that people use machines is of key importance. The most significant advances in computer science in the coming decade will be those facilitating this interaction. However, in their public discussions of the project, the researchers often equate improved interaction with the development of human-like systems. Moto-oka says (1982, p. 27): "Its greatest feature will be that interface between man and computer will greatly approach the human level.... Man will be able to communicate with computers by using speech, natural languages, pictures or images..." The report predicts that fifth generation machines will be able to understand normal speech, with a vocabulary of over 10,000 words by 1990.

There is an error in assuming that success will follow the path of artificial intelligence. The key to design lies in understanding the readiness-to-hand of the tools being built, and in anticipating the breakdowns that will occur in their use. A system that provides a limited imitation of human facilities will intrude with apparently irregular and incomprehensible breakdowns. On the other hand, we can create tools that are designed to make the maximal use of human perception and understanding without projecting human capacities onto the computer.

3. **Is the key the development of 'intelligent' systems?** Here is the weakest link in the chain. There will be many specialized uses for 'expert' systems, but they are not the basis for dealing with the human-machine interface. To a large extent, the fifth generation report uses 'intelligent' in the loose manner of phrases like 'intelligent terminals.' We find mention of 'intelligent interface functions,' 'intelligent systematization support,' 'intelligent programming,' 'intelligent VLSI designing,' 'intelligent utility system,' 'intelligent software tools,' and 'intelligent communication system.' Often this is simply an advertising slogan for a more advanced and comprehensive version of what is available now. As the project proceeds, current artificial intelligence techniques will find their way into a variety of niches

within the project, but will not be central to its overall goal of making the machine more accessible. More ambitious AI goals such as general-purpose machine translation and real natural-language understanding will be dropped.

4. **Can expert systems make effective use of specialized machines?** Much of the academic interest in the project has been generated by the attempt to make use of higher-level programming languages based on formal logic,[7] and to integrate them with mechanisms for logical inference and for efficient access to large data bases. Such languages and mechanisms are notoriously inefficient on current computers, and one of the major technical claims of the project is that new computer designs will get rid of this bottleneck.

This book is not the place for detailed technical arguments at this level. It seems likely researchers will develop more efficient devices for doing certain kinds of symbolic manipulation, particularly when dealing with large bodies of stored data. These devices will be useful for the development of specialized AI systems, and more generally in building programs operating in systematic domains, as discussed in Chapter 12. However, they will not be the panacea that ties together the rest of the goals in the chain, and it is not even obvious that the particular choices anticipated at this point will be the right ones for the more limited goals.

5. **Is parallel processing critical to new machines?** This is again a technical issue, and one on which there is broad agreement within the computer science community. It is not obvious that the particular approach currently envisioned by the project is the best one, but it will not be surprising if an effort of the anticipated magnitude leads to important new advances in this area.

6. **Is it crucial to develop advanced VLSI techniques?** Like the previous item, this is hardly a debatable point. Every major computer company and computer science laboratory is working in this area, and it is reasonable to believe that the fifth generation project can participate effectively in this line of research. The important point is that these last two areas are likely to lead to successful results that bear only a minimal relationship to the higher-level goals.

The grandiose goals, then, will not be met, but there will be useful spinoffs. In the long run, the ambitions for truly intelligent computer

---

[7]Initially the Japanese researchers plan to use PROLOG (which stands for PROgramming in LOGic), a language developed in Europe. This is considered a starting point from which new languages and systems will develop.

systems, as reflected in this project and others like it around the world, will not be a major factor in technological development. They are too rooted in the rationalistic tradition and too dependent on its assumptions about intelligence, language, and formalization.

PART III

Design

Chapter 11

Management and conversation

The preceding chapters have examined the current understanding of computers and the predictions for 'intelligent' machines and their uses. We have argued that artificial intelligence is founded on assumptions that limit its potential to generate new designs. The basic question we come back to in our concluding chapters is "What can people do with computers?" and to begin with, "What do people do?"

There is no one answer to this question. 'Doing' is an interpretation within a background and a set of concerns. People talk and walk and breathe and move their hands. They live and love and look for approval. Without a more specific orientation, the question "What do people do?" is meaningless. We are concerned with the design of new computer-based tools, and this leads us to asking what people do in a domain of linguistic action. As our primary example we consider what people do in their work, taking the office as the prototypical workplace. The issues of commitment and coordinated action that are highlighted in that setting are vital to all kinds of work situations and to 'home life' as well.

Within the office we will focus our attention more specifically on what goes on under the general category of 'management.' In referring to management, we are not limiting our concern to the running of businesses. Anyone in a position to direct actions that affect the economic, political, or physical conditions of others is in some sense a manager. In all but the most routinized jobs, a worker functions in some ways as a manager, requesting and initiating actions that affect the work of others. We will show later how an essential part of all work in organizations is the dimension of 'coordination' that is highlighted in the manager's job. We therefore begin our examination of what people do by looking at a particular person: a manager in an office.

The question "What is this person doing now?" can be answered in many domains:

- sitting at a desk sipping coffee and moving a pencil over a piece of paper.

- writing English text.

- looking for the right word to finish a sentence.

- drafting an inter-office memo.

- reminding an administrative assistant about next week's meeting concerning the software contract.

- deciding whether the marketing manager should attend the meeting.

- working on preparations for the new contract.

- trying to increase the efficiency of how this office handles contracts.

- ...

These are all appropriate descriptions, each generated in a particular domain of actions and breakdowns. As we showed in our discussion of word processing in Chapter 1, current designs for 'office automation' are based on domains dealing with the preparation of text and the manipulation of 'electronic paper,' such as memos. New tools can be designed to operate in the domain of speech acts and conversation—the one in which terms like 'reminding,' 'requesting,' and 'agreeing' are relevant. We will argue that this is the most fruitful domain for understanding and facilitating management. Every manager is primarily concerned with generating and maintaining a network of conversations for action—conversations in which requests and commitments lead to successful completion of work.

11.1   Management and decision making

In talking about managers, we are deliberately avoiding the commonly used label 'decision makers.' The managers (and by extension, other workers) we describe might be called decision makers, but that term carries a particular pre-understanding of what such a person does. We want to challenge that pre-understanding. We will first lay out the tradition of 'decision making,' and show how it can be a restrictive and misleading way of understanding what managers do.

Chapter 2 briefly reviewed the approach to decision making developed by Simon and others, which was a key starting point for the field of artificial intelligence. Simon characterizes making a decision as a heuristic search among alternatives in a problem space of possible courses of action, with the aim of achieving a preferred set of consequences. It is a process of bounded rationality, in which choices are made by applying formal rules to partial information in ways that are precise but not based on a simple model of deduction and proof. Such processes have been taken by researchers in artificial intelligence as the basis for a wide variety of human mental activity, as we saw in Chapter 8. It is not surprising, then, that the theoretical understanding developed in the earlier chapters should be applicable to the problems of management and decision making as well.

A variety of crucial questions need to be asked about the decision making model: Is this really the only way to be rational? What about other ways of coping with hesitations, such as learning and behaving according to authority, rules, or intuition? A number of secondary questions also come to mind: Where do alternatives come from? Where do preferences come from? Who is considering them? Is it not possible that a wrong way of looking at problems may drive us to find solutions to overly narrow understandings of situations?

The taken-for-granted assumption that identifies rational decision making with choosing is highly restrictive. It does not lead us to see irrationality in a situation as manifested in wrong alternatives and wrong preferences. Although it is often helpful to use methods for evaluating and choosing among alternatives, these methods are harmful when they blind us to a larger realm of concern for human behavior. Two issues are immediately apparent: thrownness in a situation, and the importance of background. We will look at these in turn.

First, the description of decision making as a heuristic search in a space of possibilities does not fit observations of what goes on in management situations. Keen and Scott-Morton (*Decision Support Systems*, 1978, p. 15) argue, "A serious weakness of the whole study of management has been ignorance of, and lack of interest in, how decisions are really made." They draw an analogy:

> Suppose on a clear day, driving a car down a suburban street at 20 mph, we see a small child running across the road in front of the car. The problem is clear—some action must be taken or the child will be hit. There are perhaps four alternatives: (1) cut off the engine, (2) put the car in reverse, (3) swerve, or (4) hit the brakes. The choice among these alternatives has been 'programmed' into us and under normal conditions we would automatically use the brakes. Change the conditions

to driving on the turnpike in pouring rain at 55 mph with traffic on all sides, and a large dog suddenly dashing across the road in front of us—to hit the dog might result in the car turning over, to swerve might result in hitting the cars on either side of us, to hit the brakes too hard might result in skidding, and so on. The careful evaluation of these alternatives by, for example, looking around to see how close the nearest car is, is a theoretical possibility only if there is sufficient time, but the high speed of the car precludes all these information-gathering activities. Thus we have a situation in which all of the variables are known but where there is is not enough time to do the evaluation. In such a case we argue that the context makes this an unstructured problem. Managers are often irritated by the tendency of management scientists to focus on the inherent structure of a decision, as in our example of driving, ignoring the context that makes that irrelevant. — Keen and Scott-Morton, *Decision Support Systems* (1978), p. 94.

This driver is an example *par excellence* of the thrownness that Heidegger points out in our everyday life. We do not act as a result of consideration, but as a way of being. The driver's reaction in this situation cannot be adequately described in terms of rationality, even bounded rationality. His habits or his experience of a prior accident may be much more important than any of his concepts or evaluations of risk. Managers are 'irritated' because the decision-making approach is based on the assumption that these 'performance limitations' are somehow peripheral or avoidable, and that a manager should be able to act without them. The theorists may succeed in convincing them of the benefits of systematic evaluation of choices, but their experience confirms Heidegger.

The problem is not just one of limitations. The view of management as rational problem solving and decision making fails to deal with the question of background. Saying that a manager is optimizing some value by choosing among alternatives for action is like regarding language understanding as a process of choosing among formal definitions. The hard part is understanding how the alternatives relevant to a given context come into being. The critical part of problem solving lies in formulating the problem.

The bounded rationality approach does not assume that a decision maker can evaluate all alternatives, but it takes for granted a well-defined problem space in which they are located. It is not clear for what observer this space of alternatives exists. In describing the behavior of a manager we (as observers) can formalize the situation by describing it as a set of alternatives with associated properties. In doing so we impose our own pre-understanding to create distinct alternatives out of the full situation. In order to write a computer program we are forced to do this kind of analysis *a priori.*

Keen and Scott-Morton (1978, p. 58) point out: "Most, if not all, of the managers' key decisions tend to be fuzzy problems, not well understood by them or the organization, and their personal judgment is essential." A problem is created by the linguistic acts in which it is identified and categorized. Of course, some situation is previous to the formulation, but its existence as a particular problem (which constrains the space of possible solutions) is generated by the commitment in language of those who talk about it. This conversation in turn exists within their shared background in a tradition.

As with language in general, we cannot look to simple notions of truth and deduction. The 'energy crisis' was not created by commercial acts of the oil companies, the Arabs, or the American consumer, but by those with the power to create consensus who looked at a long-term situation and declared it to be a crisis. The relevant question is not whether it is 'true' or 'false' that there is a problem, but what commitments are generated (for speaker and hearer) by the speech acts that created it, and how those commitments generate the space of possible actions.

11.2 Decision making and resolution

Instead of talking about 'decisions' or 'problems' we can talk of 'situations of irresolution,' in which we sense conflict about an answer to the question "What needs to be done?" If someone hires a new employee or signs a new contract, there may or may not be a 'decision,' but one can certainly say "A resolution has been reached." The process of reaching resolution is characteristically initiated by some claim that generates a mood of irresolution. Claims may be of many different kinds and origins: a routine internal evaluation, some external fact or contingency, or a new proposal, which presents us with the issue of our possibilities. The ensuing irresolution is not a process in which purely logical alternatives come to be considered. In general, there is a dissatisfaction about "where things are going," more or less articulately expressed. It is concerned with the past as a pattern of actions, and the future as potential for further actions.

The question "What needs to be done?" arises in a breakdown, in which the course of activity is interrupted by some kind of 'unreadiness.' It is often manifested in hesitation and confusion, and is *always already* oriented to a certain direction of possibilities. This pre-orientation of possibilities appears as an exclusionary bias, revealing a space of possible actions and simultaneously concealing others.

Let us illustrate with a simple example:

> You have been commuting to work in your old Chevrolet. Recently you have had to jump-start it three times, and there has been an ominous scraping sound every time you apply the brakes. One morning as you are driving to work you cannot get it into first gear. You take it to a mechanic who says there is a major problem with the transmission. Clearly you are in a situation of irresolution. You talk to your husband and decide that there are several alternatives—you can have the old car repaired, or you can buy a used or a new car. If you want a used car you can try to get it through friends or newspaper ads, or you can go to a dealer. If you get a new one you may want a van you can use for camping trips, but you're not sure you can afford it and still go on the vacation you had planned. In fact you're not sure you can afford a new car at all, since you have to keep up the payments and insurance on your husband's car as well.

From the point of view of classical decision theory, the task is to lay out the space of alternatives and to assign valuations to each. This includes dealing with the uncertainties, such as not knowing how much the repair will cost, how much trouble it will be to find a good used car, and what your financial situation will be in the future. In addition it requires comparing factors that are not directly comparable. How important is it to be able to go camping in comfort? How bad is it to be stuck with car payments that make the budget a hassle every month? What would it mean to give up the vacation? How valuable is it to avoid the increased worry about breakdowns that comes with a used car? How do you feel about being seen driving an old clunker?

The problem is not just that it is impossible to apply systematic decision techniques, but that there is a bias inherent in formulating the situation as one of choosing between these alternatives. Imagine that on the next day (since you can't drive to work) you call and check the city buses and find one you can take. After a few days of taking the bus you realize you didn't really need the car. The problem of "How can I get a working car?" has not been *solved*, it has been *dissolved*. You realize that the problem you really wanted to solve was "How can I get to work?"

Of course one might argue that you failed to identify the real space of alternatives, but that it existed nevertheless. But imagine a slightly different scenario. The bus ride takes too long, and you are complaining about the situation to your friend at work. He commiserates with you, since his bicycling to work is unpleasant when it rains. The two of you come up with the idea of having the company buy a van for an employee car pool. In this case, resolution comes in the creation of a new alternative. The issue is not one of choosing but of generating. Or, on the other hand, you might steal a car, or set up housekeeping in a tent in your office, or commit suicide. Each in its own way would 'solve the problem.' We are seriously misled if we consider the relevant space of alternatives to be the space of all logical possibilities. Relevance always comes from a pre-orientation within a background.

You talk to another friend who has just gotten his car back from the shop. He hears your story and expresses surprise at the whole thing. It never occurred to him to do anything except have it fixed, just as he always did. For him the resolution of having it repaired was not a decision. A breakdown of irresolution never occurred. This exclusionary feature is the principal element of resolution. It is sometimes articulated as reasons or arguments, in which some of the excluded paths can be pointed out ("I can't afford to buy a new car"). But there is always more that is not articulated, falling back into the fathomless background of obviousness.

This kind of exclusionary commitment is present even in situations where we do not experience irresolution; we simply act, order, promise, declare, or decline to commit ourselves to some acts. It is naive to believe that these are not rational actions, on the grounds that the process of deliberation (in the sense of choosing among alternatives) is missing. Commitment to an action, with exclusion of other possibilities, is the common feature of the processes that precede action.

We call the process of going from irresolution to resolution 'deliberation.' The principal characteristic of deliberation is that it is a kind of conversation (in which one or many actors may participate) guided by questions concerning how actions should be directed. Sometimes we can specify conditions of further inquiry to attain a resolution. On other occasions the resolution will come from a more prolonged hesitation and/or debate. Only in some of these cases will the phenomenon of choosing between alternatives occur, and a process of ranking according to some metric or other criterion may occur even less frequently.

We can describe the conversation that constitutes deliberation in the following terms:

1. At some moment in the process of articulating the claims, some incipient partial proposals can be discerned, as different people give opinions, suggestions, disparagements, counter-offers, etc. In this conversation, distinctions between means and goals, parts and wholes are discarded in favor of interpretations about possible causal links, potential results, and inconveniences.

2. At some moment, a sedimented opinion about possible courses of action to be evaluated and considered may begin to appear; this is

when the process called 'choosing' could be considered. However, the name 'choosing' is inadequate, because it suggests algorithmic procedures for selecting the course of action.

It is worth noting that much of what is called problem solving does not deal with situations of irresolution, but takes place within the normal state of resolution. For example, when a linear programming model is used to schedule operations in a refinery, the 'problem' to be solved does not call for a resolution. Resolution concerns the exploration of a situation, not the application of habitual means.

11.3   Organizations as networks of commitments

In asking "What do managers do?" we must look at what goes on in an organization as a whole. In Part I we saw that a certain kind of 'recurrence,' or repetitive pattern of actions, pervades our life as patterns of breakdown repeat themselves. An organization attempts to exploit this by division of labor, in order to be ready to deal with a breakdown as something already known.

Varying our simple car example, imagine that it is a delivery truck, not a personal car. In this case the company has a standard procedure for repair, so that the resolution of the situation is predetermined: take it into the company garage and get a temporary replacement. Other patterns of action in the organization are designed to anticipate rather than cope with breakdown—in this case, obviously, the preventive maintenance done to the trucks on a regular basis.

The concepts of breakdown and recurrence apply equally when we look beyond those areas like vehicle maintenance where they are superficially obvious. Breakdowns are not just situations of trouble, but are how concerns appear to each member of the organization. Many of them are already anticipated in the form of work specialization: standard forms to be filled out, rules for credit, policies about the levels of inventories, and so forth. To be in business is to know how to deal with breakdowns, and to be pre-oriented in anticipation of them.

The taken-for-granted recurrence in an organization includes, for example, the definitions of what products and services are to be offered and to whom, as well as what kinds of requests will be considered. The rigidity implied by this recurrence is necessary, but it also brings a danger, an inertia or bias, with a field of possibilities that tends to be narrow and closed. This rigidity is often apparent in support activities, such as maintenance and data processing. The development of means to achieve them may come to hide the purposes they were intended to serve. The blindness can take on immense proportions when the survival of an organization is assured by some external declaration, as with public bureaucracies or armies in peacetime. It becomes attached to programs and projects, attending to recurrent requests, with little sensitivity to the consequences and implications of its activity or to the declared commitments of the organization.

Decision making, as described in the first section of this chapter, is part of the recurrent activity. The professional discipline of 'systems analysis' has focussed on routine structured processes, frequently attacking problems of volume and routine rather than problems of communication. If we look carefully at the process of resolution described above, we see that the key elements are the conversation among the affected parties and the commitment to action that results from reaching resolution. Success cannot be attributed to a decision made by a particular actor, but only to the collective performance.

Careful observers of what successful managers do (such as Mintzberg, in *The Nature of Managerial Work*, 1973) have remarked that their activities are not well represented by the stereotype of a reflecting solitary mind studying complex alternatives. Instead, managers appear to be absorbed in many short interactions, most of them lasting between two and twenty minutes. They manifest a great preference for oral communication—by telephone or face to face. We may say that managers engage in conversations in which they create, take care of, and initiate new commitments within an organization. The word 'management' conveys the sense of active concern with action, and especially with the securing of effective cooperative action. At a higher level, management is also concerned with the generation of contexts in which effective action can consistently be realized.

In understanding management as taking care of the articulation and activation of a network of commitments, produced primarily through promises and requests, we cover many managerial activities. Nevertheless, we also need to incorporate the most essential responsibilities of managers: to be open, to listen, and to be the authority regarding what activities and commitments the network will deal with. These can be characterized as participation in 'conversations for possibilities' that open new backgrounds for the conversations for action.

The key aspect of conversations for possibilities is the asking of the questions "What is it possible to do?" and "What will be the domain of actions in which we will engage?" This requires a continuing reinterpretation of past activity, seen not as a collection of past requests, promises, and deeds in action conversations, but as interpretations of the whole situation—interpretations that carry a pre-orientation to new possibilities for the future. Like the car owner in our example, the manager needs to be continually open to opportunities that go beyond the previous horizon.

11.4   Decision support systems

Those who predict the development of intelligent computers propose that they be used to enhance human decision making by suggesting alternatives, predicting consequences, and pulling together the information that goes into making decisions:

> ... in the future, artificial intelligence could produce power-
> ful assistants who manage information for us, reading books,
> newspapers, magazines, reports; preparing summaries, avoid-
> ing those things the computer knows won't interest us, keeping
> abreast of everything that happens in the world, seeing that
> nothing we really should know about escapes us. These in-
> telligent computers could analyze the decisions that face us,
> searching libraries of knowledge for facts that will help with a
> decision and then presenting us with suggested courses of ac-
> tion and the probable consequences. They could understand
> specialized knowledge and know how to put it to work in some
> of the highly skilled areas in which we humans function—law
> and medicine, for example. — Stockton, "Creating computers to
> think like humans" (1980), p. 41.

It should be clear by this point that a computer cannot "see that nothing we really should know about escapes us." However, the more modest claim that a computer can help explore pre-constrained sets of alternatives has been the basis for the development of a family of tools known as 'decision support systems.' As with so-called 'expert systems,' there is both an appropriate domain of activities for such tools, and a danger in seeing them as doing too much. We will describe them here as a potential and will then contrast them to the additional kinds of tools we envision for supporting work in the domain of conversation.

> Decision Support Systems (DSS) represent a point of view on
> the role of the computer in the management decision making
> process. Decision support implies the use of computers to:
>
> 1. Help managers in their decision processes in semi-struc-
>   tured tasks.
>
> 2. Support, rather than replace, managerial judgment.

3. Improve the effectiveness of decision making rather than
its efficiency. — Keen and Scott-Morton, *Decision Support
Systems* (1978), p. 1.

In their careful definition of such systems, Keen and Scott-Morton
introduce terms that deserve more explanation. They refer to 'semi-
structured tasks' and distinguish 'effectiveness' from 'efficiency.'

Nearly every writer on management and decision making draws a di-
chotomy between two kinds of managerial situations: 'programmed vs.
nonprogrammed decision' (Simon, *The Shape of Automation for Men and
Management,* 1965), 'structured vs. unstructured problems' (Keen and
Scott-Morton, 1978), 'established vs. emergent situations' (Boguslaw, *The
New Utopians,* 1965). On the one hand there are obviously recurrent tasks,
such as the scheduling of jobs on the machines in a shop. On the other,
there are the open-ended innovative actions introduced in conversations
for possibilities.

For structured tasks it is often possible to create a set of rules and
have computers apply them to the situation. For unstructured tasks such
rules cannot be formulated. However, there is an in-between area of 'semi-
structured' tasks with some degree of recurrence but not so much that
one can fully specify the relevant rules. Keen and Scott-Morton see this
as the relevant area for computer aid to human decision making. They
state their goal not as 'efficiency' but 'effectiveness'—measured in terms
of global outcomes rather than of the speed of making decisions or their
immediate payoffs. A system is effective if an organization using it finds itself in a better position. A system can be ineffective but be highly efficient
at making decisions that are in fact (because of the particular blindness
inherent in their formulation) irrelevant or harmful to the enterprise.

We will not try to examine decision support systems in detail here. It
is clear that in day-to-day management there are areas where such tools
can be of use, and there have been many ideas for their design. However
it is important to point out some of the dangers that potentially attend
their use.

Orientation to choosing. The phrase 'decision support' carries with it
a particular orientation to what the manager does—one that we have been
criticizing. The emphasis implicit in this approach serves to reinforce the
decisionist perspective and to support a rigid status quo in organizations,
denying the validity of more social, emotive, intuitive, and personalized
approaches to the complex process of reaching resolution.

Assumption of relevance. Once a computer system has been installed,
it is difficult to avoid the assumption that the things it can deal with are

the most relevant things for the manager's concern. An information system dedicated to collecting data and answering predetermined questions, even one as well-designed as possible, will be harmful if it is not complemented by heterodox practices and a permanent attitude of openness to listening.

Unintended transfer of power. In the design of a system that will be used in an organization, many choices are made that will have significant consequences for life within that organization. As Boguslaw points out:

> A designer of systems, who has the de facto prerogative to spec-
> ify the range of phenomena that his system will distinguish,
> clearly is in possession of enormous degrees of power.... It is
> by no means necessary that this power be formalized through
> the allocation of specific authority.... It is in this sense that
> computer programmers, the designers of computer equipment,
> and the developers of computer languages possess power. To
> the extent that decisions made by each of these participants in
> the design process serve to reduce, limit, or totally eliminate
> action alternatives, they are applying force and wielding power
> in the precise sociological meaning of these terms. — Boguslaw,
> *The New Utopians* (1965), p. 190.

Often those who are invisibly empowered have an overall orientation not shared by others within the organization. Trained professionals in computer technology tend to place high values on efficiency and predictability, and to devalue the need for human discretion and innovation. The resulting design can erode the effectiveness of the organization while concentrating on its efficiency. In one case, the scheduling of jobs within a machine shop (previously done by a manager who walked around from worker to worker) was automated with a computer communication system. Only after many breakdowns was it realized that the manager in his perambulations was doing much more than simply assigning tasks. His openness to new concerns (both from talking to the workers and from his observations of the workplace) played a critical role in anticipating breakdowns, which had not been recognized in the design of the computer system.

Unanticipated effects. Every technological advance brings with it unanticipated effects, some desirable and some undesirable. In this era of ecological consciousness it is hardly necessary to give examples of dangerous unintended effects of such apparently beneficial devices as automobiles and nuclear power plants. Computer technology brings its own kinds of problems. For example, in the attempt to provide better information to managers about what was going on in one grocery warehouse, a system was installed that made it possible to monitor the activity of individual workers on a minute-by-minute basis. The workers went on strike, demanding removal of the system because of the stress it placed on them and the resulting deterioration of working conditions.

Effects of this kind can be difficult to formulate or test precisely. For example, in evaluating the dangers of large data bank systems, Wessel notes:

> Indeed, the damage resulting from the potential misuses of facts is far less serious than that which stems from the individual's simple knowledge that the data bank exists, an awareness which has a subtle but inevitable effect on how he conducts himself. — Wessel, *Freedom's Edge* (1974), p. 30.

Obscuring responsibility. Once a computer system is designed and in place, it tends to be treated as an independent entity. The understanding we have been developing leads us to recognize the computer's role not as a surrogate expert, but as an intermediary—a sophisticated medium of communication. A group of people (normally including both computer specialists and experts in the subject domain) build a program incorporating a formal representation of some of their discourse. The computer transmits consequences of their statements to users of the system, typically combining these statements. The fact that these combinations involve complex deductive logic, heuristic rule application, or statistical analysis does not alter the basic structure of communicative acts.

Once we recognize the machine as an intermediary, it becomes clear that the commitment inherent in the use of language is made by those who produce the system. In the absence of this perspective it becomes all too easy to make the dangerous mistake of interpreting the machine as making commitments, thereby concealing the source of responsibility for what it does. Medical diagnosis programs (which can be thought of as decision support systems for physicians) provide a good example. Imagine a program written by a team of computer specialists working with a group of medical experts, installed by the administration of a hospital, and used by a member of the medical house staff in choosing a treatment. If the diagnosis was wrong and the patient is harmed, who is responsible?

The problem may not be one of wrong medical knowledge, but rather one of background assumptions. An answer that is correct in one context may be inappropriate in another. For example, if the program was written with ambulatory patients in mind, it might not be appropriate for a chronic bedridden invalid. A person writing a program (or contributing to its 'knowledge base') does so within a background of assumptions about how the program will be used, and how its responses will be interpreted. Part of this can be made explicit in documentation, but part is an implicit background of what can be normally understood. Except for systems operating within strongly constrained domains, there inevitably comes a breakdown because the system is being used in a way that does not fit the assumptions. In a computer-mediated system (as opposed to direct personal interaction), it is difficult to maintain the implicit commitments and the potential for a dialog in the face of breakdown.

False belief in objectivity. One immediate consequence of concealing commitment is an illusion of objectivity. Since the 'facts' stored by a computer cannot be readily associated with a commitment by an individual who asserted them, it is easy to be blind to the nature of their origin. Evans, for example, argues in describing the computer projections of the future world economy done for the Club of Rome (*The Limits to Growth*, 1972):

> Like it or not, even the most ardent anti-computerist would admit that the computer, lacking emotions, hunches and prejudices, would consider and generate only the stark facts of the matter. — Evans, *The Micro Millennium* (1979), p. 92.

But this is nonsense. Computers neither consider nor generate facts. They manipulate symbolic representations that some person generated on the belief that they corresponded to facts. There was a good deal of hindsight analysis of the disastrous results for the U.S. military in Vietnam produced by the faith placed by commanders in computer analyses that were based on highly distorted and even fabricated 'facts.' The issue, though, is not just one of mistake or of conscious fabrication. It is in the nature of any 'fact' that it is an assertion by an individual in a context, based on a background of pre-understanding. D'Amato illustrates the fallacy of ignoring this in his discussion of computer aids in law:

> Another possible benefit is that law might seem more impartial to the man on the street if computers were to take over large areas now assigned to judges. There is certainly some degree of belief on the part of the public that judges cannot escape their own biases and prejudices and cannot free themselves from their relatively privileged class position in society. But computers, unless programmed to be biased, will have no bias. — D'Amato, "Can/should computers replace judges?" (1977), p. 1300.

Once again this is utter nonsense. In order for a program to be biased, it is not necessary for the programmer to consciously set out to insert prejudices, nor is he or she likely to do this. In order even to begin the task of preparing a program, a programmer (or legal expert working with the programmer) must operate within his or her own background of prejudice. This is not a mistake that can be avoided, but an essential condition for knowledge of any kind. To repeat a central quotation from Gadamer:

> It is not so much our judgments as it is our prejudices that constitute our being.... the historicity of our existence entails that prejudices, in the literal sense of the word, constitute the initial directedness of our whole ability to experience. Prejudices are biases of our openness to the world. They are simply conditions whereby we experience something—whereby what we encounter says something to us. — Gadamer, *Philosophical Hermeneutics* (1976), p. 9.

To conclude, we see decision support systems, like all computer-based systems, as offering a potential for new kinds of human action. With this potential come particular blindnesses and dangers. The question is not whether such systems are good or bad, but how our understanding and use of them determines what we do and what we are.

11.5 Tools for conversation

We have been arguing that the domain of 'decision support'—dealing with alternatives, valuations, and choice—is not the most promising domain in which to build computer tools for managing. In this section, we will outline another kind of computer tool, based on the theory of management and conversation we have been developing. We begin by reviewing the basic points of the theory, as developed in this chapter and in Chapter 5:

1. Organizations exist as networks of directives and commissives. Directives include orders, requests, consultations, and offers; commissives include promises, acceptances, and rejections.

2. Breakdowns will inevitably occur, and the organization needs to be prepared. In coping with breakdowns, further networks of directives and commissives are generated.

3. People in an organization (including, but not limited to managers) issue utterances, by speaking or writing, to develop the conversations required in the organizational network. They participate in the creation and maintenance of a process of communication. At the core of this process is the performance of linguistic acts that bring forth different kinds of commitments.

In fulfilling an organization's external commitments, its personnel are involved in a network of conversations. This network includes requests and promises to fulfill commitments, reports on the conditions of fulfillment of commitments, reports on external circumstances, declarations of new policies, and so on. The organization encounters requests and other external contingencies that it can deal with by making commitments that can be fulfilled by the activation of certain special *networks of recurrent conversations*, where only certain details of the content of the conversations differ, not their general structure. These networks of recurrent conversations are the core of organization. They are embodied as intercommunicating offices, each specialized in fulfilling certain kinds of commitments.

A person working within an organization is always concerned with questions such as "What is missing?", "What needs to be done?", and "Where do I stand in terms of my obligations and opportunities?" In situations where many people must act together, the problem of coordination becomes a crucial one. For many organizations it is a matter of survival. The networks of commitments and the conversations in which people participate are becoming larger and more complex, and the complexity of organizations has gone beyond the point where it can be controlled without appropriate tools.

New computer-based communication technology can help anticipate and avoid breakdowns. It is impossible to completely avoid breakdowns by design, since it is in the nature of any design process that it must select a finite set of anticipations from the situation. But we can partially anticipate situations where breakdowns are likely to occur (by noting their recurrence) and we can provide people with the tools and procedures they need to cope with them. Moreover, new conversational networks can be designed that give the organization the ability to recognize and realize new possibilities.

Many systems designed by computer professionals are intended to facilitate the activity of an individual working alone. Although such tools (including word processors, filing systems, program creation aids, etc.) are useful, they leave out the essential dimension of collective work. In most work environments the coordination of action is of central importance. The conversational dimension permeates every realm of coordinated activity, whether it be computer programming, medical care, or selling shoes. The details differ from setting to setting, but there is a common theoretical basis and a common regular structure. Computer-based tools can be used in requesting, creating, and monitoring commitments. They can provide relevant answers to the question "What do I need to do?", or as we prefer to put it, "What is the status of my active commitments?"

The rules of conversation are not arbitrary conventions like the rules of chess, but reflect the basic nature of human language and action. The taxonomy of speech acts and the diagram of conversation structure presented in Chapter 5 deal with the fundamental ontology of linguistic acts. They provide a basis for the design of tools to operate in a linguistic domain.

We are not proposing that a computer can 'understand' speech acts by analyzing natural language utterances. It is impossible to formulate a precise correspondence between combinations of words and the structure of the commitments listened to in a conversation. What we propose is to make the user aware of this structure and to provide tools for working with it explicitly. Substantial experience is being amassed with a computer program that we have developed called "The Coordinator^{TM} Workgroup Productivity System."[1] It is the first example of a new class of products that we are calling "coordination systems" or "workgroup systems," for use on computer communication networks (which might be based on local networks, time-sharing, or advanced telephone exchanges) to which all of the participants have access through some kind of workstations. Its objective is to make the interactions transparent—to provide a ready-to-hand tool that operates in the domain of conversations for action.

There are a surprisingly few basic conversational building-blocks (such as request/promise, offer/acceptance, and report/acknowledgement) that frequently recur in conversations for action. The development of a conversation requires selection among a certain finite set of possibilities that is defined by the opening directive and the subsequent responses. It is like a dance, giving some initiative to each partner in a specific sequence.

A coordination system supports a number of operations:

Speech act origination. An individual performs a speech act using a system such as The Coordinator by: selecting the illocutionary force from a small set of alternatives (the basic building blocks mentioned above); indicating the propositional content in text; and explicitly entering temporal relationships to other (past and anticipated) acts. By specifying directly, for example, that a particular utterance is a 'request' with a specific date for satisfaction, the listening is constrained to a much greater degree than it is for an English sentence such as "Would you be able to..." The force of a speech act comes from concerned listening, and by making an explicit declaration of this force we can avoid confusion and breakdown due to differences (intended or unintended) in the listening of the concerned parties. In addition to having a direct specification of its force, a speech act is related to others, for example as the response to a request, or

---

[1]For a more developed description of coordination systems, see Flores and Ludlow, "Doing and speaking in the office" (1981), Flores, "Management and communication in the office of the future" (1982), and Winograd, "A language/action perspective on the design of cooperative work" (1987). "The Coordinator" is a registered trademark of Action Technologies, Inc.

as a request being made in order to satisfy some previous commitment. These relationships are made explicit in the way a speech act is entered into the workstation. The need to select among pre-structured alternatives for possible illocutionary forces serves as a kind of 'coaching' that reveals the space of possibilities and the structure of different acts within it.

Monitoring completion. Much of the moment-by-moment concern of language is directed towards the completion of conversations for action. The questions "What do I have to do now?" and "What do I need to check up on?" are really questions about the movement of conversations towards states of completion (which may or may not include satisfaction of the initial request), as described in Chapter 5. A coordination system can keep track of where things stand and when they will change. This can be used to generate reminders and alerts and to provide a clear picture of what is happening and where potential breakdowns lie ahead.

Keeping temporal relations. A coordination system can keep track of time relationships within the network and use them to help anticipate and cope with breakdowns. Time is not an incidental condition, but a critical aspect of every speech act. A promise is not really a promise unless there is a mutually understood (explicitly or implicitly) time for satisfaction. More subtly, a request is not fully formed unless there is a time specified for reply and for completion. In unstructured social settings, these time conditions are understood by the participants through their shared background and may never be made explicit. In structured organizations they are stated directly, and in situations like contract negotiations they are dealt with in the law. As speech acts are made using the system, the user is coached to explicitly represent the temporal relations that are central to the network of commitment. These relations can be used to monitor what needs to be done and to warn of potential breakdowns.

Examination of the network. An individual can display part of the conversation network, showing the conversations and their status, the individual commitments and requests, and their relationships to others. It is possible, for example, to find out what requests were generated in anticipation of breakdown in satisfying a particular commitment, or what requests are still awaiting a response from a particular individual. The details of the interaction (for example using a graphic display) are important for making the tool ready-to-hand, but are not theoretically central. The key is that the network is observed in the space generated by the structure of conversation.

Automated application of recurrence. Every organization deals with situations that recur and are handled in a standard way. For example, if a certain request (e.g., for payment) has not been met within a certain time, other requests are made (to the same party or others). A coordination system can be given this pattern and trigger the corresponding acts without direct intervention. It is important to remember that it is never the computer that makes a request or commitment. A person can specify a recurrent request or commitment, instances of which are generated automatically.

Recurrence of propositional content. So far we have not described the propositional content of the speech acts. This is an intentional strategy, in that the crucial dimension of conversation for coordination is the illocutionary content and its attendant temporal relations. But of course there are recurrences of propositional content as well. A 'purchase order' or 'travel advance request' or any other such form is designed to facilitate the generation of a request or commitment dealing with a particular content. The creation and use of 'forms' of this kind can be integrated into a coordination system, within the framework provided by the basic conversation.

Another system that illustrates some of the opportunities, possible constructions, and applications of coordination systems was described by Cashman and Holt ("A communication-oriented approach to structuring the software maintenance environment," 1980). It was one part of a distributed programming environment for maintaining large software collections. As the software being maintained by the system was distributed and used, people needed to fix bugs, make improvements, and produce updated versions. This process was extremely difficult to manage, leading to long delays and failure to meet the needs of software users. By providing a computer tool to maintain the structure of the requests and commitments, they were able to greatly improve productivity. Other such systems are in development at a number of institutions.[2]

In using a coordination system, the individual is faced with a restricted set of possibilities. It is not the same as a face-to-face conversation, a telephone call, or even an electronic message. Because the illocutionary forces and temporality are specified explicitly, it is necessary to be conscious of them and to have a mutually visible manifestation of them. This is valuable in a wide variety of everyday communications within organizations, but it is not a universal communicating device, equally applicable to all

---

[2]See, for example, Holt, Ramsey, and Grimes, "Coordination system technology as the basis for a programming environment" (1983), and Sluzier and Cashman, "XCP: An experimental tool for supporting office procedures" (1984).

situations. In many contexts this kind of explicitness is not called for, and may even be detrimental. Language cannot be reduced to a representation of speech acts. A coordination system deals with one dimension of language structure—one that is systematic and crucial for the coordination of action, but that is part of the larger and ultimately open-ended domain of interpretation.

We conclude here by pointing out that computer tools themselves are only one part of the picture. The gain from applying conversation theory in organizations has to do with developing the communicative competence, norms, and rules for the organization, including the training to develop the appropriate understanding. This includes the proper terminology, skills, and procedures to recognize what is missing, deteriorated, or obtruding (i.e., what is broken-down), and the ability to cope with the situation.

People have experience in everyday dealing with others and with situations. Nevertheless, there are different levels of competence. Competence here does not mean correct grammatical usage or diction, but successful dealing with the world, good managerial abilities, and responsibility and care for others. Communicative competence means the capacity to express one's intentions and take responsibilities in the networks of commitments that utterances and their interpretations bring to the world. In their day-to-day being, people are generally not aware of what they are doing. They are simply working, speaking, etc., more or less blind to the pervasiveness of the essential dimensions of commitment. Consequently, there exists a domain for education in communicative competence: the fundamental relationships between language and successful action. People's conscious knowledge of their participation in the network of commitment can be reinforced and developed, improving their capacity to act in the domain of language.

Chapter 12

Using computers:
A direction for design

This book is concerned with the design of computer-based systems to facilitate human work and interaction. In this final chapter we suggest directions for the future, drawing on the discourse developed in Part I to re-examine some basic questions about what designing means.

The most important designing is *ontological*.[1] It constitutes an intervention in the background of our heritage, growing out of our already-existent ways of being in the world, and deeply affecting the kinds of beings that we are. In creating new artifacts, equipment, buildings, and organizational structures, it attempts to specify in advance how and where breakdowns will show up in our everyday practices and in the tools we use, opening up new spaces in which we can work and play. Ontologically oriented design is therefore necessarily both reflective and political, looking backwards to the tradition that has formed us but also forwards to as-yet-uncreated transformations of our lives together. Through the emergence of new tools, we come to a changing awareness of human nature and human action, which in turn leads to new technological development. The designing process is part of this 'dance' in which our structure of possibilities is generated.

The concluding sections of this chapter will discuss the ontical-ontological significance of design—how our tools are part of the background in which we can ask what it is to be human. First we consider the direct relevance of our theoretical orientation to the design of computer systems. We

---

[1] We do not use 'design' here in the narrow sense of a specific methodology for creating artifacts, but are concerned with a broad theory of design like that sought in the work of reflective architects such as Alexander (*Notes on the Synthesis of Form*, 1964).

will use coordination systems, such as The Coordinator^{TM} described in Chapter 11, as our primary example. But our intended scope is larger, encompassing other computer systems and ultimately all technology.

12.1   A background for computer design

In the popular literature on computers, one frequently encounters terms such as 'user-friendly,' 'easy-to-learn,' and 'self-explaining.' They are vague and perhaps overused, but they reflect real concerns—concerns that are not adequately understood within the rationalistic tradition, and to which phenomenological insights about readiness-to-hand, breakdown, and blindness are relevant.

Readiness-to-hand

One popular vision of the future is that computers will become easier to use as they become more like people. In working with people, we establish domains of conversation in which our common pre-understanding lets us communicate with a minimum of words and conscious effort. We become explicitly aware of the structure of conversation only when there is some kind of breakdown calling for corrective action. If machines could understand in the same way people do, interactions with computers would be equally transparent.

This transparency of interaction is of utmost importance in the design of tools, including computer systems, but it is not best achieved by attempting to mimic human faculties. In driving a car, the control interaction is normally transparent. You do not think "How far should I turn the steering wheel to go around that curve?" In fact, you are not even aware (unless something intrudes) of using a steering wheel. Phenomenologically, you are driving down the road, not operating controls. The long evolution of the design of automobiles has led to this readiness-to-hand. It is not achieved by having a car communicate like a person, but by providing the right coupling between the driver and action in the relevant domain (motion down the road).

In designing computer tools, the task is harder but the issues are the same. A successful word processing device lets a person operate on the words and paragraphs displayed on the screen, without being aware of formulating and giving commands. At the superficial level of 'interface design' there are many different ways to aid transparency, such as special function keys (which perform a meaningful action with a single keystroke), pointing devices (which make it possible to select an object on the screen), and menus (which offer a choice among a small set of relevant actions).

More important is the design of the domains in which the actions are generated and interpreted. A bad design forces the user to deal with complexities that belong to the wrong domain. For example, consider the user of an electronic mail system who tries to send a message and is confronted with an 'error message' saying "Mailbox server is reloading." The user operates in a domain constituted of people and messages sent among them. This domain includes actions (such as sending a message and examining mail) that in turn generate possible breakdowns (such as the inability to send a message). Mailbox servers, although they may be a critical part of the implementation, are an intrusion from another domain—one that is the province of the system designers and engineers. In this simple example, we could produce a different error message, such as "Cannot send message to that user. Please try again after five minutes." Successful system builders learn to consider the user's domain of understanding after seeing the frustrations of people who use their programs.

But there is a more systematic principle at stake here. The programmer designs the language that creates the world in which the user operates. This language can be 'ontologically clean' or it can be a jumble of related domains. A clearly and consciously organized ontology is the basis for the kind of simplicity that makes systems usable. When we try to understand the appeal of computers like the Apple MacIntosh (and its predecessor the Xerox Star), we see exactly the kind of readiness-to-hand and ontological simplicity we have described. Within the domains they encompass—text and graphic manipulation—the user is 'driving,' not 'commanding.' The challenge for the next generation of design is to move this same effectiveness beyond the superficial structures of words and pictures into the domains generated by what people are doing when they manipulate those structures.

Anticipation of breakdown

Our study of Heidegger revealed the central role of breakdown in human understanding. A breakdown is not a negative situation to be avoided, but a situation of non-obviousness, in which the recognition that something is missing leads to unconcealing (generating through our declarations) some aspect of the network of tools that we are engaged in using. A breakdown reveals the nexus of relations necessary for us to accomplish our task. This creates a clear objective for design—to anticipate the forms of breakdown and provide a space of possibilities for action when they occur. It is impossible to completely avoid breakdowns by means of design. What can be designed are aids for those who live in a particular domain of breakdowns. These aids include training, to develop the appropriate understanding of the domain in which the breakdowns occur and also to develop the skills and procedures needed to recognize what has broken down and how to cope with the situation.

Computer tools can aid in the anticipation and correction of breakdowns that are not themselves computer breakdowns but are in the application domain. The commitment monitoring facilities in a coordination system are an example, applied to the domain of conversations for action. In the design of decision support systems, a primary consideration is the anticipation of potential breakdowns. An early example of such a system was Cybersyn,[2] which was used for monitoring production in a sector of the economy of Chile. This system enabled local groups to describe the range of normal behavior of economic variables (such as the output of a particular factory), and to be informed of significant patterns of variation that could signal potential breakdown.

But more importantly, breakdowns play a fundamental role in design. As the last section pointed out, the objects and properties that constitute the domain of action for a person are those that emerge in breakdown. Returning to our simple example of an electronic mail system, our 'fix' left a person with certain courses of action in face of the breakdown. He or she can simply forget about sending the message or can wait until later to try sending it again. But it may be possible to send it to a different 'mail server' for delayed forwarding and delivery. If so, it is necessary to create a domain that includes the existence of mail servers and their properties as part of the relevant space in which the user exists.

In designing computer systems and the domains they generate, we must anticipate the range of occurrences that go outside the normal functioning and provide means both to understand them and to act. This is the basis for a heuristic methodology that is often followed by good programmers ("In writing the program try to think of everything that could go wrong"), but again it is more than a vague aphorism. The analysis of a human context of activity can begin with an analysis of the domains of breakdown, and that can in turn be used to generate the objects, properties, and actions that make up the domain.

The blindness created by design

Any opening of new possibilities closes others, and this is especially true of the introduction of technology. As an example, consider the possibility of an 'electronic library' in which one can search for items using sophisticated cataloging techniques based on publication information (such as author, publisher, and title) and topic classifications (such as the Library of Congress categories and the key word systems used in many journals).

---

[2]Cybersyn is described in Beer, *Platform for Change* (1975).

If we accept the domain generated by those classifications as the relevant one for finding books, the system is appropriate and useful. However, this may not be the right choice. The facility may make it easier for a reader to find a book on a specific narrow topic, while reducing the ease of 'browsing' through shelves of loosely related material. Recognizing the importance of background and thrownness, it becomes clear that the unexpected and unintended encounters one has in browsing can at times be of much greater importance than efficient precise recall. If the problem is narrowly construed as "Find a book, given specific information" then the system may be good. If we put it into its larger context of "Find writings relevant to what you want to do" it may well not be, since relevance cannot be formalized so easily. In providing a tool, we will change the nature of how people use the library and the materials within it.

As with breakdown, blindness is not something that can be avoided, but it is something of which we can be aware. The designer is engaged in a conversation for possibilities. Attention to the possibilities being eliminated must be in a constant interplay with expectations for the new possibilities being created.

12.2   A design example

We turn now to a concrete example of how our theoretical background might guide the design of a computer-based system in a practical setting. It is not a complete analysis of the specific case, but is a vehicle for suggesting possibilities and clarifying the points in these two concluding chapters. We have chosen a mundane business example, but the same principles hold for applications of computers in all kinds of organizations.

> *The setting:* You have been operating a successful dress shop for several years and expanded last year to a chain of three stores. You have not made any use of computers, but have recently come to feel they might be of some help. Profits aren't what they should be, you are losing some customers who seem dissatisfied with the service they get, and the staff feels overworked.

There are no clear problems to be solved: Action needs to be taken in a situation of irresolution.

This is the typical case in which questions about what to do arise, as described in Chapter 11. There is no clear 'problem' to be solved, but a sense of irresolution that opens opportunities for action. Computers are not the 'solution,' but may be useful in taking actions that improve the

situation. Once the manager senses this, the typical next step would be
to go to computer service vendors to find out what kinds of 'systems' are
available and to see if they are worth getting. The space of possibilities
is determined by the particular offerings and the 'features' they exhibit.
But we can begin with a more radical analysis of what goes on in the store
and what kinds of tools are possible.

**A business (like any organization) is constituted as a network of
recurrent conversations.**

As a first step we look for the basic networks of conversation that constitute the business. We ask "Who makes requests and promises to whom,
and how are those conversations carried to completion?" At a first level
we treat the company as a unity, examining its conversations with the
outside world—customers, suppliers, and providers of services. There are
some obvious central conversations with customers and suppliers, opened
by a request for (or offer of) dresses in exchange for money. Secondary
conversations deal with conditions of satisfaction for the initial ones: conversations about alteration of dresses, conversations concerning payment
(billing, prepayment, credit, etc.), and conversations for preventing breakdown in the physical setting (janitorial services, display preparation, etc.).

Taking the business as a composite, we can further examine the conversational networks among its constituents: departments and individual
workers. There are conversations between clerk and stockroom, clerk and
accounting, stockroom and purchasing, and so forth. Each of these conversation types has its own recurrent structure, and plays some role in
maintaining the basic conversations of the company. As one simple example, consider the conversation in which the stock clerk requests that
purchase orders be sent to suppliers. Instances of this conversation are either triggered by a conversation in which a salesperson requested an item
that was unavailable, or when the stock clerk anticipates the possibility of
such a breakdown. Other conversations are part of the underlying structure that makes possible the participation of individuals in the network
(payroll, work scheduling, performance evaluations, etc.). Each conversation has its own structure of completion and states of incompletion with
associated time constraints.

**Conversations are linked in regular patterns of triggering and
breakdown.**

The goal in analyzing these conversations is a description in which the
linkages between the recurrent conversations are made explicit. These
links include normal triggering (e.g., a customer request triggers a stock

request), and others that deal with breakdown (e.g., if a request for alteration is not met on time it may trigger a request by the customer to see the manager). Having compiled this description, we can see possibilities for restructuring the network on the basis of where conversations fail to be completed satisfactorily. We may, for example, note that customer dissatisfaction has come from alterations not being done on time (perhaps because alterations are now being combined for the three stores and therefore the tailors aren't immediately available). Actions might include imposing a rigid schedule for alterations (e.g., never promise anything for less than a week) so that commitments will be met on time, even if the times that can be promised are less flexible. Or it might mean introducing better tools for coordination, such as a computer-based system for keeping track of alteration requests and giving more urgent ones higher priority.

In creating tools we are designing new conversations and connections.

When a change is made, the most significant innovation is the modification of the conversation structure, not the mechanical means by which the conversation is carried out (e.g., a computer system versus a manual one based on forms). In making such changes we alter the overall pattern of conversation, introducing new possibilities or better anticipating breakdowns in the previously existing ones. This is often not noticed because the changes of devices and of conversation structure go hand in hand. At times the changes can be beneficial, and at times detrimental. There are many cases of systems for activities like job scheduling that were introduced to make things more efficient, but as a result of modifying the conversation structure they in fact hindered the work. Often this is the result of taking one part of the conversation network (the 'official' or 'standard' part) and embodying it in the structure of the computer system, thereby making impossible other less frequent types of requests and promises that are crucial for anticipating and coping with breakdowns. When we are aware of the real impact of design we can more consciously design conversation structures that work.

As an example, there is a potential for coordination systems to reduce the need for rigid work schedules. Much of the temporal structure of what goes on in organizations is driven by the need to be able to anticipate completion. If the manager knows that a certain task will be done every Friday, then he or she can make a commitment to do something that uses its results on the following Monday. For many routine tasks, this is the best way to guarantee effective coordination. But it can also be an inflexible straitjacket that reduces the space of possibilities open to workers in organizing their activities. If effective coordination on a conversation-by-conversation basis could be regularized, then the rigidity could be relaxed, altering the conversation structure to make the workers more productive.

Design includes the generation of new possibilities.

No analysis of existing recurrent structures is a full account of the possibilities. The existing networks represent a particular point of structural coupling of the organization to the world in which it exists. Actions may radically alter the structure. In our example, the store might simply stop doing alterations. Or it might hire more tailors, or contract out the alterations, or hire many more tailors and go into the contract alteration business as well. In some cases, the business as a whole may have a new interpretation. The owner of a small candy store notes the success of the video games in the back, and may ultimately decide that the business is a video game parlor with a candy counter. No methodology can guarantee that all such possibilities will be found, but a careful analysis of the conversation structure can help reveal conversations with a potential for expansion.

In designing computer-based devices, we are not in the position of creating a formal 'system' that covers the functioning of the organization and the people within it. When this is attempted, the resulting system (and the space of potential action for the people within it) is inflexible and unable to cope with new breakdowns or potentials. Instead we design additions and changes to the network of equipment (some of it computer-based) within which people work. The computer is like a tool, in that it is brought up for use by people engaged in some domain of action. The use of the tool shapes the potential for what those actions are and how they are conducted. The computer is unlike common tools in its connectivity to a larger network of equipment. Its power does not lie in having a single purpose, like a carpenter's plane, but in its connection to the larger network of communication (electronic, telephone, and paper-based) in which organizations operate.

Domains are generated by the space of potential breakdown of action.

If our dress shop owner chooses to install a computer-based system dealing with some of the conversations, the analysis proceeds by examining (and generating) the appropriate domains. Much computer automation deals with standard derived domains, such as payroll accounting, billing, and employee scheduling. A domain of relevant objects, properties, and actions has already been generated through standard practice, and is enforced by the need to satisfy external conversations based on it (such as those with the Internal Revenue Service). But even in these sedimented cases, it is important to recognize that ultimately the present-at-hand world of objects is always based on the breakdown of action.

As an obvious example, we can ask what a customer's 'address' is. The immediate response is "For what?" (or, "What is the conversation in which it determines a condition of satisfaction?"). There are two distinct answers. Some conversations with customers involve requests for the physical transfer of goods while others involve correspondence. Different conditions of satisfaction require different kinds of address. This is a standard case, and most business forms and computer data bases will distinguish "shipping address" and "billing address." But we may also need an address where the person can be found during the day to perform further measurements. In every case, the relevant 'property' to be associated with the person is determined by the role it plays in an action. This grounding of description in action pervades all attempts to formalize the world into a linguistic structure of objects, properties, and events.

This also leads us to the recognition that the development of any computer-based system will have to proceed in a cycle from design to experience and back again. It is impossible to anticipate all of the relevant breakdowns and their domains. They emerge gradually in practice. System development methodologies need to take this as a fundamental condition of generating the relevant domains, and to facilitate it through techniques such as building prototypes early in the design process and applying them in situations as close as possible to those in which they will eventually be used.

Breakdown is an interpretation—everything exists as interpretation within a background.

As a somewhat more interesting example of how the world is generated by language, consider the conditions of satisfaction associated with 'fit.' The customer is only satisfied by a dress that fits, and a complex linguistic domain (the domain of clothing sizes) has been generated to provide a means of anticipating and preventing breakdown. But 'fitting' cannot be objectively defined. One person may be happy with an article that someone else of the same overall shape and size would reject. The history of fashion and the differences between cultures make it clear that 'fitting' is an interpretation within a particular horizon. But at the same time it is not purely individual. The background shared by a community is what makes individual 'tastes' possible.

Ultimately, then, satisfaction is determined not by the world but by a declaration on the part of the requestor that a condition is satisfied. The case of 'fit' may seem extreme, but every condition of satisfaction ultimately rests on a declaration by an individual, within the background of a community. The cases that seem 'objective' are those in which there is great regularity and for which possible conversations about satisfaction have been regularized (perhaps formally in the legal system). One kind of innovation lies in generating new interpretations and corresponding new domains for conditions of satisfaction. In fact, one might view this as the primary enterprise of the 'fashion' industry (and of every entrepreneur).

Domains of anticipation are incomplete.

The domain of clothing sizes was generated to anticipate breakdown in the satisfaction of conversations in which clothing is sold. It is a useful but incomplete attempt. Given the interpretive nature of 'fit,' no system of sizes can guarantee success. Once again, this is a clearly visible example of a more universal phenomenon. Every attempt to anticipate breakdown reflects a particular domain of anticipation. This does not make it useless, but means that we must design with the flexibility to encounter other (always unanticipated) breakdowns.

As another case, consider inventory control. The stock clerk tries to maintain a supply on hand that will decrease the possibility of running out, while keeping the overall investment in inventory as low as feasible (thereby anticipating breakdowns in cash flow). Orders are sent far enough ahead of time to anticipate delivery lags, and counts of what has been sold are used to keep track of what is on hand. But of course there are breakdowns in all of this. A supplier can simply fail to deliver as promised. An inventory count based on previous inventory and on what has been sold fails to account for the items lost through shoplifting. This does not mean that anticipation is impossible or that systems should not be built to do it. The critical part is to recognize clearly what the real domains are. An inventory count is not a statement of fact, but a declaration of an interpretation. For many purposes this can be treated as though it were the 'actual number of items,' but conversations that depend on this assumption will fail to deal with the unexpected cases.

Computers are a tool for conducting the network of conversations.

Most of what has been said in this section is independent of computers. It applies to businesses and organizations, whether they operate with the most modern equipment or with ledger pads and quills. It is also not a prescription for what they should do, but an analysis of what they are already doing. If we examine what computers are doing now in settings like our example, we find them embodying possibilities for action within a set of recurrent conversations. Whether it be a payroll system, a billing system, or an inventory control system, the hardware and software are a medium in which requests and promises are made and monitored. There is a wide range of possibilities, including the standard packages now prominent in commercial applications, the decision support and coordination systems described in Chapter 11, and the 'expert' systems being widely promoted today. In each case, the question to be asked is not an abstract one of "What kind of system is needed?" but a concrete one of how different tools will lead to new conversations and in the end to new ways of working and Being. 'Computerization' in its pejorative sense occurs with devices that were designed without appropriate consideration of the conversational structures they engender (and those that they consequently preclude).

Innovations have their own domains of breakdown.

We have not tried to deal in our dress shop example with concrete questions of computer devices. In practice one needs to make many choices based on the availability, utility, and cost of different kinds of equipment—computers, software packages, networks, printers, and so on. In doing so, all of the same theoretical considerations apply. As computer users know all too well, breakdown is a fundamental concern. It is important to recognize in this area that breakdowns must be understood within a larger network of conversation as well. The issue is not just whether the machine will stop working, but whether there is a sufficient network of auxiliary conversations about system availability, support, training, modification, and so on. Most of the well-publicized failures of large computer systems have not been caused by simple breakdowns in their functioning, but by breakdowns in this larger 'web of computing'[3] in which the equipment resides.

Design is always already happening.

Imagine yourself in the situation depicted at the beginning of the section. You resolve to take actions that will lead to acquiring and installing a new computer system. What does our analysis have to offer? Aren't the available computer systems good enough? What guidance is there in determining what to do or buy?

Our first response is that we are not proposing some new answer to the 'data processing problem.' Much of our theoretical analysis applies to existing systems, and many of these operate in ways that achieve what

---

[3]This term is from Kling and Scacchi, "The web of computing" (1982), which is based on empirical studies of experience with large scale computer systems in a social context.

we propose. This is not surprising, since a situation of natural selection applies—those systems that work ultimately survive.

But this is not the whole picture. It is not necessary to belabor what everyone knows from experience—computer systems are frustrating, don't really work right, and can be as much of a hindrance as a help in many situations. We don't offer a magic solution, but an orientation that leads to asking significant questions. The result of an analysis like the above might well be to lead the shop owner to make changes to the conversations as they now occur (by voice and writing) without buying a computer at all. Or it might serve as a background from which to generate criteria for deciding among competing vendors and creating new interpretations for the available systems within the particular situation. Or it might be the basis for coming up with entirely new tools that open new possibilities for action. Design always proceeds, with or without an articulated theory, but we can work to improve its course and its results.

12.3   Systematic domains

The previous sections point out the central role played by the creation through language of the domains in which we act. Language is the creation of distinctions: nouns distinguish objects into groups, verbs distinguish kinds of actions, etc. This is not something we choose to do, but is a fundamental condition of using language. Furthermore, the words are constitutive of the objects among which they distinguish. As we showed at length in Chapter 5, language does not describe a pre-existing world, but creates the world about which it speaks. There are whole domains, such as those in financial markets involving 'shares,' 'options,' and 'futures,' whose existence is purely linguistic—based on expressions of commitment from one individual to another.

The use of a distinction is very different from its explicit formal articulation. The fact that we commonly use a word does not mean that there is an unambiguous formal way to identify the things it denotes or to determine their properties. But whenever there is a recurrent pattern of breakdown, we can choose to explicitly specify a *systematic domain*, for which definitions and rules are articulated.

The preceding chapters have repeatedly contrasted the computational manipulation of formal representations with the being-in-the-world of human thought and understanding. In each case we have shown how the projection of human capacities onto computational devices was misleading. But there is a positive side to this difference. Computers are wonderful devices for the rule-governed manipulation of formal representations, and there are many areas of human endeavor in which such manipulations are crucial. In applying computers appropriately to systematic domains, we develop effective tools.

The development of systematic domains is of course not new. Mathematics is a prototypical example of such a domain, and the development of a calculus of logical form, as begun by philosophers such as Frege and Russell, made it possible to apply mathematical techniques to more general representations of objects and their properties. Work in computer science has added a new dimension—the design of mechanisms that can carry out complex sequences of symbolic manipulations automatically, according to a fixed set of rules.

There are many domains in which such manipulations are commonplace. One of the most obvious is the numbers representing financial entities and transactions. Every accounting program, payroll program, and billing program operates within a systematic domain of bookkeeping that has evolved over centuries of commercial experience. The advent of computers has not yet had a major impact on the structure of that domain, but it has made it possible to do quickly and efficiently what was previously tedious and costly.

Nobody would argue that an accounting program like Visicalc[4] 'thinks' about business, but it is a vital tool because of the clear and appropriate correspondence between its domain and the activities that generate the commercial world. Another widespread example is 'word processing,' as illustrated in our introductory chapter. Its domain is the superficial stuff of language—letters and punctuation marks, words, sentences, and paragraphs. A word processor does not 'understand' language, but can be used to manipulate text structures that have meaning to those who create and read them. The impact comes not because the programs are 'smart' but because they let people operate effectively in a systematic domain that is relevant to human work.

We can best understand the creation of expert systems as the creation of systematic domains that are relevant and useful to a particular profession. In developing such a system, there is an initial period of 'knowledge acquisition,' during which professionals in the domain work together with 'knowledge engineers' to articulate the structure of the relevant concepts and rules. This is often described as a process of 'capturing' the knowledge that the experts already have and use. In fact, it is a creative design activity in which a systematic domain is created, covering certain aspects of the professionals' work. The successful examples of expert systems have almost all been the result of long and intensive effort by a particularly qual-

---

[4]Visicalc is a microcomputer program that lets a person manipulate an 'electronic spreadsheet' with rows and columns of related figures. It is one of the most commercially successful pieces of software ever created, and is credited with motivating the purchase of more small home and business computers than any other single program.

ified practitioner, and it can well be argued that the domains generated in developing the system are themselves significant research contributions.

Such *profession-oriented domains* can be the basis for computational tools that do some tasks previously done by professionals. They can also be the basis for tools that aid in communication and the cooperative accumulation of knowledge. A profession-oriented domain makes explicit aspects of the work that are relevant to computer-aided tools and can be general enough to handle a wide range of what is done within a profession, in contrast to the very specialized domains generated in the design of a particular computer system. A systematic domain is a structured formal representation that deals with things the professional already knows how to work with, providing for precise and unambiguous description and manipulation. The critical issue is its correspondence to a domain that is ready-to-hand for those who will use it.

Examples of profession-oriented systematic domains already exist. One of the reasons for Visicalc's great success is that it gives accountants transparent access to a systematic domain with which they already have a great deal of experience—the spreadsheet. They do not need to translate their actions into an unfamiliar domain such as the data structures and algorithms of a programming language. In the future we will see the development of many domains, each suited to the experience and skills of workers in a particular area, such as typography, insurance, or civil engineering.

To some extent, the content of each profession-oriented domain will be unique. But there are common elements that cross the boundaries. One of these—the role of language in coordinated action—has already been discussed at length. The computer is ultimately a *structured dynamic communication medium* that is qualitatively different from earlier media such as print and telephones. Communication is not a process of transmitting information or symbols, but one of commitment and interpretation. A human society operates through the expression of requests and promises among its members. There is a systematic domain relevant to the structure of this network of commitments, a domain of 'conversation for action' that can be represented and manipulated in the computer.

Another widely applicable domain is the specification of mechanisms like those in computer hardware and programs. These involve physically embodied systems that can be understood as carrying out discrete processes (processes that proceed in identifiable individual steps). There are kinds of objects, properties, and relations that are suited to describing them and that can be embodied in a systematic domain. Programming languages are one approach to formalizing this domain, but in general they are not well suited to the communication of intent and conceptual structure. They are too oriented to the structure of the machine, rather than to the structure of its behavior. We are beginning to see the development of 'system specification languages'[5] that deal with the domain of computational devices in a more general way.

In all situations where systematic domains are applicable, a central (and often difficult) task is to characterize the precise form and relevance of the domain within a broader orientation. In our example of coordination systems, we find the embedding of a systematic domain (conversation structure) within the larger domain of language. The meaning of an utterance is not captured by a formal structure, but lies in the active listening of a hearer in a context. At the same time, its role within a particular network of requests and promises can be identified and represented in a systematic way. In a similar vein, the rows and columns of a bookkeeping program do not reflect the meaning of the economic system, but isolate one aspect that is amenable to systematic treatment. The limitations of this domain become obvious in attempts to apply accounting techniques to non-systematic areas, such as measuring overall 'productivity' or providing a cost-benefit analysis of activities (such as research) whose 'products' are not easily measured.

Even within areas such as law—where there is a primary concern with the social and ethical fabric—we find an interaction between the contextual and the systematic. The statutes and decisions provide a systematic framework that is the basis for argumentation in court. There are clear formal statements, such as "In order to be guilty of first-degree murder, there must be premeditation." But of course these rest on understandings of terms like 'premeditation,' which call for contextual interpretation. Computer programs can help a lawyer manipulate formal structures and the deductions that can be made from them, while leaving the 'hard questions' open to human interpretation.[6]

12.4 Technology and transformation

Our book has focussed on the designing of computer-based tools as part of a larger perspective of ontological design. We are concerned with what happens when new devices are created, and with how possibilities for innovation arise. There is a circularity here: the world determines what we can do and what we do determines our world. The creation of a new device or systematic domain can have far-reaching significance—it can create new ways of being that previously did not exist and a framework for actions that would not have previously made sense. As an example, systematic bookkeeping techniques did not just make it easier to keep track of the

---

[5]See Winograd, "Beyond programming languages" (1979).

[6]See Gardner, *An Artificial Intelligence Approach to Legal Reasoning* (in press), for an example and a general discussion of the issues.

financial details of business as it existed. New ways of doing business (in fact, whole new businesses dealing with financial transactions) became possible, and the entire financial activity of society evolved in accord with the structure of the new domain.

The hermeneutic orientation of Chapter 3 and the biological theories of Chapter 4 give us insight into this process. In the act of design we bring forth the objects and regularities in the world of our concern. We are engaged in an activity of interpretation that creates both possibilities and blindness. As we work within the domain we have defined, we are blind to the context from which it was carved and open to the new possibilities it generates. These new possibilities create a new openness for design, and the process repeats in an endless circle.

In Maturana's terms, the key to cognition is the plasticity of the cognitive system, giving it the power of structural coupling. As the domain of interactions is modified, the structure of the interacting system changes in accord with it. We cannot directly impose a new structure on any individual, but whenever we design changes to the space of interactions, we trigger changes in individual structure—changes to the horizon that is the precondition for understanding.

Computers have a particularly powerful impact, because they are machines for acting in language. In using them we engage in a discourse generated within the distinctions set down by their programmers. The objects, properties, and acts we can distinguish and perform are organized according to a particular background and pre-understanding. In most cases this pre-understanding reflects the rationalistic tradition we have criticized throughout this book. It includes biases about objectivity, about the nature of 'facts' (or 'data' or 'information') and their origin, and about the role of the individual interacting with the computer.

We have argued that tools based on this pre-understanding will lead to important kinds of breakdown in their use. But there is a larger problem as well. As we work with devices whose domains of action are based on an interpretation of 'data,' 'goals,' 'operators,' and so forth, we develop patterns of language and action that reflect these assumptions. These carry over into our understanding of ourselves and the way we conduct our lives. Our criticism of descriptions of human thought as 'decision making' and language understanding as the manipulation of representations is not just a prediction that certain kinds of computer programs will fail. It reflects a deeper concern with the discourse and actions that are generated by a rationalistic interpretation of human action. Computer systems can easily reinforce this interpretation, and working with them can reinforce patterns of acting that are consistent with it.[7]

---

[7]This effect is described in Turkle, *The Second Self* (1984).

On the other hand, where there is a danger there is an opportunity. We can create computer systems whose use leads to better domains of interpretation. The machine can convey a kind of 'coaching' in which new possibilities for interpretation and action emerge. For example, coordination systems grew out of research on how to train people to improve their effectiveness in working with others. This training in 'communication for action'[8] reveals for people how their language acts participate in a network of human commitments. The training does not involve computers, but rests on the development of a new linguistic domain—new distinctions and descriptions that serve as a basis for action. The use of a coordination system can help develop and reinforce this new understanding. Even at the simple level of providing the initial possibilities of 'make request' and 'make promise' instead of 'send message,' it continually reminds one of the commitment that is the basis for language. As one works successfully in this domain, the world begins to be understood in these terms, in settings far away from the computer devices.

This is just one example of a phenomenon that is only beginning to emerge in designing computers—the domain created by a design is a domain in which people live. Computers, like every technology, are a vehicle for the transformation of tradition. We cannot choose whether to effect a transformation: as designers and users of technology we are always already engaged in that transformation, independent of our will. We cannot choose what the transformation will be: individuals cannot determine the course of a tradition. Our actions are the perturbations that trigger the changes, but the nature of those changes is not open to our prediction or control. We cannot even be fully aware of the transformation that is taking place: as carriers of a tradition we cannot be objective observers of it. Our continuing work toward revealing it is at the same time a source of concealment.

However, we can work towards unconcealment, and we can let our awareness of the potentials for transformation guide our actions in creating and applying technology. In ontological designing, we are doing more than asking what can be built. We are engaging in a philosophical discourse about the self—about what we can do and what we can be. Tools are fundamental to action, and through our actions we generate the world. The transformation we are concerned with is not a technical one, but a continuing evolution of how we understand our surroundings and ourselves—of how we continue becoming the beings that we are.

---

[8]The training was developed by F. Flores through Hermenet, Inc., in San Francisco, and Logonet, Inc., in Berkeley.

Bibliography

Alexander, Christopher, *Notes on the Synthesis of Form*, Cambridge, MA: Harvard University Press, 1964.

Alexander, Tom, Computers on the road to self-improvement, *Business Week*, June 14, 1982, 148-160.

Alvey, Lord, *A Programme for Advanced Information Technology: The Report of the Alvey Committee*, London: Her Majesty's Stationery Office, 1982.

Austin, J.L., *How to Do Things with Words*, Cambridge, MA: Harvard University Press, 1962.

Barnett, G. Octo, The computer and clinical judgment, *The New England Journal of Medicine*, 307:8 (August 19, 1982), 494-495.

Barwise, Jon and John Perry, *Situations and Attitudes*, Cambridge, MA: Bradford/M.I.T. Press, 1983.

Beer, Stafford, *Platform for Change*, New York: Wiley, 1975.

Begley, Sharon, John Carey and Michael Reese, How smart can computers get?, *Newsweek* 95:26 (June 30, 1980), 52-53.

Betti, Emilio, *Teoria Generale della Interpretazione*, Milan: Dott. A. Giuffre, 1955.

Bobrow, Daniel, Dimensions of representation, in Bobrow and Collins (1975), 1-34.

Bobrow, Daniel (Ed.), Special issue on non-monotonic logic, *Artificial Intelligence*, 13:1 (January 1980), 1-174.

Bobrow, Daniel and Allen M. Collins (Eds.), *Representation and Understanding: Studies in Cognitive Science*, New York: Academic Press, 1975.

Bobrow, Daniel and Donald Norman, Some principles of memory schemata, in Bobrow and Collins, (1975), 131-150.

Bobrow, Daniel and Terry Winograd, An overview of KRL, a knowledge representation language, *Cognitive Science,* 1:1 (January 1977), 3-46.

Bobrow, Daniel and Terry Winograd, KRL: Another perspective, *Cognitive Science,* 3:1 (January-March 1979), 29-42.

Bobrow, Daniel, Terry Winograd, and the KRL Research Group, Experience with KRL-0: One cycle of a knowledge representation language, *Proceedings of the Fifth International Joint Conference on Artificial Intelligence*, Pittsburgh: Carnegie Mellon Computer Science Department, 1977, 213-222.

Boguslaw, Robert, *The New Utopians: A Study of System Design and Social Change*, Englewood Cliffs, NJ: Prentice Hall, 1965.

Buchanan, Bruce, New research on expert systems, in J.E. Hayes, D. Michie, and Y-H. Pao (Eds.), *Machine Intelligence 10*, Chichester: Ellis Horwood Ltd., 1982, 269-299.

Business Week, Artificial Intelligence; The second computer age begins, March 8, 1982, 66-72.

Business Week, Robots join the labor force, June 9, 1980, 62-76.

Cadwallader-Cohen, J.B., W.S. Zysiczk, and R.R. Donnelly, The chaostron, *Datamation*, 7:10 (October 1961). Reprinted in R. Baker (Ed.), *A Stress Analysis of a Strapless Evening Gown*, New York: Anchor, 1969.

Cashman, Paul M. and Anatol W. Holt, A communication-oriented approach to structuring the software maintenance environment, *ACM SIGSOFT, Software Engineering Notes*, 5:1 (January 1980), 4-17.

Chomsky, Noam, *Reflections on Language*, New York: Pantheon, 1975.

Cicourel, Aaron V., *Cognitive Sociology: Language and Meaning in Social Interaction*, New York: Free Press, 1974.

Club of Rome, *The Limits to Growth*, New York: Universe Books, 1972.

CNSRS, Report on artificial intelligence, prepared by the Inria Sico club and the CNSRS working party on Artificial Intelligence, in *Technology and Science of Informatics*, 2:5 (1983), 347-362.

D'Amato, Anthony, Can/should computers replace judges?, *Georgia Law Review*, 11 (1977), 1277-1301.

Davidson, Donald and G. Harman (Eds.), *Semantics of Natural Language*, Dordrecht: Reidel, 1972.

Davis, Dwight B., Assessing the Strategic Computing Initiative, *High Technology*, 5:4 (April 1985), 41-49.

Davis, Randall, Interactive transfer of expertise: Acquisition of new inference rules, *Artificial Intelligence*, 12:2 (August 1979), 121-157.

Dennett, Daniel, Intentional systems, *The Journal of Philosophy*, 68 (1971), 87-106. Reprinted in Haugeland (1981), 220-242.

Dennett, Daniel, Mechanism and responsibility, in Ted Honderich (Ed.), *Essays on the Freedom of Action*, London: Routledge and Kegan Paul, 1973. Reprinted in D. Dennett, *Brainstorms: Philosophical Essays on Mind and Psychology*, Montgomery, VT: Bradford, 1978, 233-255.

Dreyfus, Hubert L., *What Computers Can't Do: A Critique of Artificial*

Reason, New York: Harper & Row, 1972 (2nd Edition with new Preface, 1979).

Dreyfus, Hubert L., *Being-in-the-World: A Commentary on Division I of Heidegger's Being and Time*, Cambridge, MA: M.I.T. Press, in press.

Dreyfus, Hubert L., and Stuart E. Dreyfus, *Mind Over Machine*, New York: Macmillan/The Free Press, 1985.

Evans, Christopher, *The Micro Millennium*, New York: Viking, 1979.

Feigenbaum, Edward, AAAI President's message, *AI Magazine*, 2:1 (Winter 1980/81), 1, 15.

Feigenbaum, Edward and Julian Feldman (Eds.), *Computers and Thought*, New York: McGraw Hill, 1963.

Feigenbaum, Edward and Pamela McCorduck, *The Fifth Generation: Artificial Intelligence and Japan's Computer Challenge to the World*, Reading, MA: Addison-Wesley, 1983.

Fillmore, Charles, An alternative to checklist theories of meaning, in A. Cogen et al. (Eds.), *Proceedings of the First Annual Meeting of the Berkeley Linguistics Society*, University of California, Berkeley, 1975.

Flores, C. Fernando, Management and communication in the office of the future, Report printed by Hermenet Inc., San Francisco, 1982.

Flores, C. Fernando and Juan Ludlow, Doing and speaking in the office, in G. Fick and R. Sprague (Eds.), *DSS: Issues and Challenges*, London: Pergamon Press, 1981.

Fodor, Jerry, Methodological solipsism considered as a research strategy in cognitive psychology, *The Behavioral and Brain Sciences*, 3 (1980), 63-73. Reprinted in Haugeland (1981), 307-338.

Fogel, Lawrence J., Alvin J. Owens, and Michael J. Walsh, *Artificial Intelligence Through Simulated Evolution*, New York: John Wiley, 1966.

Frege, Gottlob, On sense and nominatum, in H. Feigl and W. Sellars (Eds.), *Readings in Philosophical Analysis*, New York: Appleton Century Crofts, 1949, 85-102 (published originally in German, 1892).

Gadamer, Hans-Georg, *Truth and Method* (translated and edited by Garrett Barden and John Cumming), New York: Seabury Press, 1975.

Gadamer, Hans-Georg, *Philosophical Hermeneutics* (translated by David E. Linge), Berkeley: University of California Press, 1976.

Gardner, Anne, *An Artificial Intelligence Approach to Legal Reasoning*, Cambridge, MA: Bradford/M.I.T. Press, in press.

Gardner, Howard, *The Mind's New Science: A History of the Cognitive Revolution*, New York: Basic Books, 1985.

Garfinkel, Harold, What is ethnomethodology, in H. Garfinkel (Ed.), *Studies in Ethnomethodology*, Englewood Cliffs, NJ: Prentice Hall, 1967.

Goffman, Erving, *The Presentation of Self in Everyday Life*, New York: Doubleday, 1959. Penguin Edition, 1971.

Grice, H. Paul, Logic and conversation, in P. Cole and J.L. Morgan (Eds.), *Studies in Syntax, Volume III,* New York: Academic Press, 1975.

Grosz, Barbara, Utterance and objective: Issues in natural language communication, *AI Magazine,* 1:1 (Spring 1980), 11-20.

Habermas, Jürgen, What is universal pragmatics?, in J. Habermas, *Communication and the Evolution of Society* (translated by Thomas McCarthy), Boston: Beacon Press, 1979, 1-68.

Habermas, Jürgen, Wahrheitstheorien, in H. Fahrenbach (Ed.), *Wirklichkeit und Reflexion,* Neske: Pfullingen, 1973, 211-265. Quotations based on anonymous translation (manuscript 40 pp.), "Theories of truth," undated.

Haugeland, John, The nature and plausibility of cognitivism, *The Behavioral and Brain Sciences,* 2 (1978), 215-260. Reprinted in Haugeland (1981), 243-281.

Haugeland, John, *Mind Design,* Montgomery, VT: Bradford/M.I.T. Press, 1981.

Haugeland, John, *Artificial Intelligence: The Very Idea,* Cambridge, MA: Bradford/M.I.T. Press, 1985.

Hayes, Pat, In defence of logic, *Proceedings of the Fifth International Joint Conference on Artificial Intelligence,* Pittsburgh: Carnegie Mellon Computer Science Dept., 1977, 559-565.

Heidegger, Martin, *Being and Time* (translated by John Macquarrie and Edward Robinson), New York: Harper & Row, 1962.

Heidegger, Martin, *What Is Called Thinking?* (translated by Fred D. Wieck and J. Glenn Gray), New York: Harper & Row, 1968.

Heidegger, Martin, *On the Way to Language* (translated by Peter Hertz), New York: Harper & Row, 1971.

Heidegger, Martin, *The Question Concerning Technology* (translated by William Lovitt), New York: Harper & Row, 1977.

Hintikka, Jaako, Quantifiers in logic and quantifiers in natural languages, in S. Koener (Ed.), *Philosophy of Logic,* Berkeley: University of California Press, 1976, 208-232.

Hintikka, Jaako, Julius Moravcsik, and Patrick Suppes (Eds.), *Approaches to Natural Language,* Dordrecht: Reidel, 1973.

Hirsch, E.D. Jr., *Validity in Interpretation,* New Haven, CT: Yale University Press, 1967.

Hobbs, Jerry, Coherence and coreference, *Cognitive Science,* 3:1 (January-March 1979), 67-90.

Hofstadter, Douglas, *Gödel, Escher, Bach: An Eternal Golden Braid,* New York: Basic Books, 1979.

Holt, Anatol W., H.R. Ramsey and J.D. Grimes, Coordination system technology as the basis for a programming environment, *Electrical Communication,* 57:4 (1983), 307-314.

Jackendoff, Ray, Toward an explanatory semantic representation, *Linguistic Inquiry*, 7:1 (Winter 1976) 89-150.

Jastrow, Robert, The thinking computer, *Science Digest*, 90:6 (June 1982), 54-55, 106-107.

John-Steiner, Vera, and Paul Tatter, An interactionist model of language development, in B. Bain (Ed.), *The Sociogenesis of Language and Human Conduct*, New York: Plenum, 1983.

Katz, J.J. and J.A. Fodor, The structure of a semantic theory, in J. Fodor and J. Katz (Eds.), *The Structure of Language*, Englewood Cliffs, NJ: Prentice Hall, 1964, 479-518.

Keen, Peter G.W. and Michael S. Scott-Morton, *Decision Support Systems: An Organizational Perspective*, Reading, MA: Addison-Wesley, 1978.

Keenan, Edward L. (Ed.), *Formal Semantics of Natural Language*, Cambridge: Cambridge University Press, 1975.

Kling, Rob and Walt Scacchi, The web of computing: Computing technology as social organization, in M. Yovits (Ed.), *Advances in Computers, Vol. 21*, 1982, 1-90.

Köhler, Wolfgang, *Gestalt Psychology*, New York: Liveright, 1929.

Kuhn, Thomas, *The Structure of Scientific Revolutions*, Chicago: University of Chicago Press, 1962.

Lakatos, Imre, Falsification and the methodology of scientific research programmes, in I. Lakatos and A. Musgrave (Eds.), *Criticism and the Growth of Knowledge*, Cambridge: Cambridge University Press, 1970.

Lakatos, Imre, *Proofs and Refutations*, Cambridge: Cambridge University Press, 1976.

Lakoff, George and Mark Johnson, *Metaphors We Live By*, Chicago: University of Chicago Press, 1980.

Land, Edwin, The retinex theory of color vision, *Scientific American*, 237:6 (December 1977), 108-128.

Leech, Geoffrey, *Towards a Semantic Description of English*, London: Longman, 1969.

Lehnert, Wendy, Michael Dyer, Peter Johnson, and C.J. Yang, BORIS: An experiment in in-depth understanding of narratives, *Artificial Intelligence*, 20:1 (1983), 15-62.

Lenat, Douglas, The ubiquity of discovery, *Artificial Intelligence*, 9 (1977), 257-286.

Lenat, Douglas, Computer software for intelligent systems, *Scientific American*, 251:3 (September 1984), 204-211.

Lindsay, Robert, Bruce Buchanan, Edward Feigenbaum, and Joshua Lederberg, *DENDRAL*, New York: McGraw Hill, 1980.

Linsky, Leonard (Ed.), *Semantics and the Philosophy of Language*, Urbana: University of Illinois Press, 1952.

Lyons, John, *Structural Semantics,* Oxford: Blackwell, 1963.

Marr, David, *Vision,* New York: Freeman, 1982.

Maturana, Humberto R., Biology of cognition (1970). Reprinted in Maturana and Varela (1980), 2-62.

Maturana, Humberto R., Neurophysiology of cognition, in P. Garvin (Ed.), *Cognition: A Multiple View,* New York: Spartan Books, 1970, 3-23.

Maturana, Humberto R., Cognitive strategies, in von Foerster (1974), 457-469.

Maturana, Humberto R., The organization of the living: a theory of the living organization, *International Journal Man-Machine Studies,* 7 (1975), 313-332.

Maturana, Humberto R., Biology of language: The epistemology of reality, in G.A. Miller and E. Lenneberg (Eds.), *Psychology and Biology of Language and Thought: Essays in Honor of Eric Lenneberg,* New York: Academic Press, 1978, 27-64.

Maturana, H.R., J.Y. Lettvin, W.S. McCulloch, and W.H. Pitts, Anatomy and physiology of vision in the frog, *Journal of General Physiology,* 43 (1960), 129-175.

Maturana, Humberto R., Gabriela Uribe, and Samy Frenk, A biological theory of relativistic color coding in the primate retina, *Arch. Biologia y Med. Exp.,* Suplemento No. 1, Santiago: University of Chile, 1968.

Maturana, Humberto R. and Francisco Varela, *Autopoiesis and Cognition: The Realization of the Living,* Dordrecht: Reidel, 1980.

McCarthy, John, An unreasonable book (review of Joseph Weizenbaum's *Computer Power and Human Reason*), *Creative Computing,* 2:9 (September-October 1976), 84-89.

McDermott, John, R1: A rule-based configurer of computer systems, *Artificial Intelligence,* 19:1 (September 1982), 39-88.

Minsky, Marvin (Ed.), *Semantic Information Processing,* Cambridge, MA: M.I.T. Press, 1967.

Minsky, Marvin, A framework for representing knowledge, in Winston (1975), 211-277.

Minsky, Marvin, The society theory of thinking, in P. Winston and R. Brown (Eds.), *Artificial Intelligence: An MIT Perspective,* Cambridge, MA: M.I.T. Press, 1979, 421-452.

Minsky, Marvin, K-Lines: a theory of memory, in Norman (1981), 87-104.

Mintzberg, Henry, *The Nature of Managerial Work,* New York: Harper & Row, 1973.

Moore, J. and A. Newell, How can MERLIN understand?, in L. Gregg (Ed.), *Knowledge and Cognition,* Baltimore, MD: Lawrence Erlbaum Associates, 1973.

Moravcsik, Julius, How do words get their meanings?, *The Journal of Philosophy,* 78:1 (January 1981), 5-24.

Moto-oka, T., Keynote speech: Challenge for knowledge information processing systems, in Moto-oka (1982), 1-89.

Moto-oka, T. (Ed.), *Fifth Generation Computer Systems: Proceedings of International Conference on Fifth Generation Computer Systems*, Amsterdam: North Holland, 1982.

Newell, Allen, The knowledge level, *Artificial Intelligence*, 18:1 (January 1982), 87-127.

Newell, Allen and Herbert A. Simon, *Human Problem Solving*, New York: Prentice Hall, 1972.

Newell, Allen and Herbert A. Simon, Computer science as an empirical inquiry: Symbols and search, *Communications of the ACM*, 19:3 (March 1976), 113-26. Reprinted in Haugeland (1981), 35-66.

Nilsson, Nils, *Learning Machines*, New York: McGraw Hill, 1965.

Nilsson, Nils, *Principles of Artificial Intelligence*, Palo Alto, CA: Tioga, 1980.

Norman, Donald A. (Ed.), *Perspectives on Cognitive Science*, Norwood, NJ: Ablex, 1981.

Norman, Donald and Daniel Bobrow, On data-limited and resource-limited processes, *Cognitive Psychology*, 7 (1975), 44-64.

Norman, Donald, David Rumelhart, and the LNR Group, *Explorations in Cognition*, San Francisco: Freeman, 1975.

Palmer, Richard E., *Hermeneutics: Interpretation theory in Schleiermacher, Dilthey, Heidegger and Gadamer*, Evanston, IL: Northwestern University Press, 1969.

Pask, Gordon, *Conversation, Cognition and Learning: A Cybernetic Theory and Methodology*, Amsterdam: Elsevier, 1975.

Pask, Gordon, *Conversation Theory: Applications in Education and Epistemology*, Amsterdam: Elsevier, 1976.

Putnam, Hilary, Is semantics possible?, in H.E. Kiefer and M.K. Munitz (Eds.), *Language, Belief and Metaphysics*, Albany: SUNY Press, 1970, 50-63.

Rosch, Eleanor, Cognitive representations of semantic categories, *Journal of Experimental Psychology: General*, 104 (1975), 192-233.

Russell, Bertrand, *Introduction to Mathematical Philosophy*, London: Allen and Unwin, 1920.

Samuel, Arthur, Some studies in machine learning using the game of checkers, in Feigenbaum and Feldman (1963), 71-108.

Schank, Roger, Language and memory, in Norman (1981), 105-146.

Schank, Roger C. and R.P. Abelson, *Scripts Plans Goals and Understanding*, Hillsdale, NJ: Lawrence Erlbaum Associates, 1977.

Schank, Roger and Christopher Riesbeck, *Inside Computer Understanding*, Hillsdale, NJ: Lawrence Erlbaum Associates, 1981.

Searle, John R., *Speech Acts,* Cambridge: Cambridge University Press, 1969.

Searle, John R., A taxonomy of illocutionary acts, in K. Gunderson (Ed.), *Language, Mind and Knowledge,* Minneapolis: University of Minnesota, 1975, 344-369. Reprinted in Searle (1979), 1-29.

Searle, John R., *Expression and Meaning: Studies in the Theory of Speech Acts,* Cambridge: Cambridge University, 1979.

Searle, John R., Literal meaning, *Erkenntnis,* 13:1 (July 1978), 207-224. Reprinted in Searle (1979), 117-136.

Searle, John R., Minds, brains, and programs, *The Behavioral and Brain Sciences,* 3 (1980), 417-424. Reprinted in Haugeland (1981), 282-306.

Shortliffe, Edward, *Computer Based Medical Consultations: MYCIN,* New York: American Elsevier, 1976.

Simon, Herbert A., *The Shape of Automation for Men and Management,* New York: Harper and Row, 1965.

Simon, Herbert A., *Administrative Behavior* (3rd Edition), New York: The Free Press, 1976.

Simon, Herbert A., Cognitive science: The newest science of the artificial, in Norman (1981), 13-26.

Sluzier, Suzanne and Paul M. Cashman, XCP: An experimental tool for supporting office procedures, *IEEE 1984 Proceedings of the First International Conference on Office Automation,* Silver Spring, MD: IEEE Computer Society, 1984, 73-80.

Stockton, William, Creating computers to think like humans (first of a two part series), *New York Times Magazine,* December 7, 1980, 40-43, 182-187.

Suppes, Patrick, From behaviorism to neobehaviorism, *Theory and Decision,* 6 (1975), 269-285.

Tarski, Alfred, The semantic conception of truth, *Philosophy and Phenomenological Research,* 4 (1944). Reprinted in Linsky (1952), 13-47.

Turkle, Sherry, *The Second Self: Computers and the Human Spirit,* New York: Simon and Schuster, 1984.

Uttal, Bro, Here comes Computer Inc., *Fortune,* October 4, 1982, 82-90.

Varela, Francisco J., *Principles of Biological Autonomy,* New York: Elsevier-North Holland, 1979.

Varela, Francisco J., Living ways of sense making: A middle way approach to neurosciences, in P. Livingston et al. (Eds.), *Disorder-Order: Proceedings of the Stanford International Symposium,* Saratoga, CA: Anma Libri, 1984.

Varela, Francisco J., *El Arbol de Conocimiento* (forthcoming). To be translated as *The Tree of Knowledge.*

von Foerster, Heinz (organizer), *Cybernetics of Cybernetics,* Urbana: Biological Computer Laboratory, University of Illinois, 1974.

Weizenbaum, Joseph, ELIZA, *Communications of the ACM,* 9:1 (January, 1966), 36-45.

Weizenbaum Joseph, *Computer Power and Human Reason,* San Francisco: Freeman, 1976.

Wessel, Milton R., *Freedom's Edge: The Computer Threat to Society,* Reading, MA: Addison-Wesley, 1974.

Winograd, Terry, *Understanding Natural Language,* New York: Academic Press, 1972.

Winograd, Terry, When will computers understand people?, *Psychology Today,* 7:12 (May 1974), 73-79.

Winograd, Terry, Toward a procedural understanding of semantics, *Revue Internationale de Philosophie,* 3:117-118 (1976), 260-303.

Winograd, Terry, Beyond programming languages, *Communications of the ACM,* 22:7 (July 1979), 391-401.

Winograd, Terry, What does it mean to understand language?, in Norman (1981), 231-264.

Winograd, Terry, Moving the semantic fulcrum, *Linguistics and Philosophy,* 8:1 (1985), 91-104.

Winograd, Terry, A language/action perspective on the design of cooperative work, *Human-Computer Interaction,* 3 (1987).

Winston, Patrick, Learning structural descriptions from examples, in Winston (1975), 157-210.

Winston, Patrick (Ed.), *The Psychology of Computer Vision,* New York: McGraw Hill, 1975.

Winston, Patrick, Learning by creating and justifying transfer frames, *Artificial Intelligence,* 10:2 (April 1978), 147-172.

Winston, Patrick, Learning and reasoning by analogy, *Communications of the ACM,* 23:12 (December 1980), 689-703.

Wittgenstein, Ludwig, *Philosophical Investigations* (translated by G.E. Anscombe), Oxford: Blackwell, 1963.

Zeleny, M. (Ed.), *Autopoiesis, a Theory of the Living Organization,* New York: Elsevier-North Holland, 1978.

Name Index

Subject Index

AAAI (*See* American Association for Artificial Intelligence)

Abstract machine, 88

Accidental representation, 91–92

Accounting, as profession oriented systematic domain, 176

Acquisition (*See* Knowledge acquisition)

Act (*See* Linguistic act, Speech act)

Action, 71–72
  and autopoiesis, 47
  breakdown of, 170–171
  conversation for (*See* Conversation for action)
  and existence, 69
  as interpretation, 144
  and language (*See* Language)
  in problem solving, 23
  and thrownness, 34, 71

Address, as example of distinction, 171

Agreement, as basis for meaning, 62–64

AI (*See* Artificial intelligence)

Aitiational scheme, 57

Algorithm, 87, 90

Alternatives, 146–149
  choice among, 20–23, 144–150, 153
  generation of, 149
  (*See also* Decision making)

Alvey committee, 134

American Association for Artificial Intelligence, 125, 128n

Amnesty International, xiv

Analogy, 68, 116–117

Analytic philosophy (*See* Philosophy)

Anticipation (*See* Breakdown)

Apple (*See* MacIntosh)

Appropriateness
  of computer response, 121
  of utterance, 57–58

Arch, as example of concept, 101

Argument, structure of, 67–68

Artificial intelligence, 3–4, 93–139
  applications, 125–131
  and background, 113
  claims for, 3–4, 152
  and cognition, 8, 25, 75, 130
  and common sense, 98
  critiques of, 16
  current developments, 125–139
  and formal logic, 85
  as paradigm, 109
  as problem solving, 22–23, 95–97
  programming for, 87–89
  and representation, 84–86, 96n, 98
  (*See also* Expert system, Fifth generation, Heuristic, Learning, Thinking, Understanding)

Assembly language, 91

194